NEUROPHILOSOPHY OF CONSCIOUSNESS VOL. IV

SPECULATIONS AND CONJECTURES.

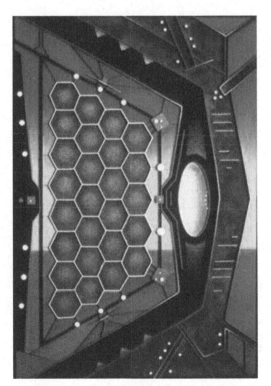

Deuterium Reactor by Tina York

Dr. Angell O. de la Sierra, Esq.

ISBN: 978-1-4669-4931-7 (sc)
ISBN: 978-1-4669-4930-0 (e)

Trafford rev. 08/01/2012

 www.trafford.com

North America & international
toll-free: 1 888 232 4444 (USA & Canada)
phone: 250 383 6864 ♦ fax: 812 355 4082

CONTENTS

CHAPTER 1

Reciprocal Transactional Information Transfer Neocortex ⟷ Transfinity

A Quantum Receptor/'Synapse' Complex?

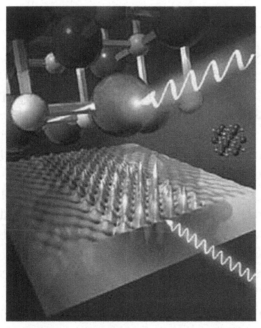

Frenkel Exciton

INTRODUCTION

Nobody seems to seriously question that the information transfer from the classical sense-phenomenal receptors to the human brain in conscious state mode is faster than the classic neuron synaptic relay would account for, notwithstanding Libet's claim to the contrary when denying free conscious will. In this brief presentation we speculate on the controversial possibility of a quantum mechanism to transfer relevant environmental information to central neurons at the speed of light thus complementing the effects of the slower classical synaptic transmission. In so doing we may provide more credible criteria on which to base allegations of reciprocal transfinite 'perceptions' otherwise known derogatorily as ESP.

We will briefly analyze the possible receptor/synaptic role that quark/nuclear particles in DNA **dark** baryonic codons (nucleotide base location?) may play when interfacing between the external environment (transfinite cosmic radiation, axions?) and intra cortical biomolecules (RNA, proteins, A-acids, etc.). This way a reciprocal transactional information exchange between the internal brain and the external transfinite environment may be realized across a putative hydrogen-magnetic flux tube[1] bridge complex which dynamically bonds (entangles) the external transfinite cosmic particle or axion → and the human brain via a transmission bridge formed by a DNA codon nuclear 'receptor' and the corresponding internal and opposite 'acceptor' nuclear/quark spin, the latter likely located in the hydrophobic milieu of the membrane or bio-molecule (where DNA 'transcription' is taking place). This way DNA may arguably act as topological quantum computer[2] controlling the reciprocal input-output information flow between the human brain and its transfinite environment during evolution.

ARGUMENTATION

For the sake of simplicity the analysis will center on the role played by the **hydrogen bond** complex between Adenine-Thymidine (A-T) and Guanosine-Cytosine (G-C) in DNA '**external** DNA codon receptor' and the equivalent brain biomolecule '**internal** acceptor', i.e., acting as a magnetic flux conveyance bridge complex between the dark baryonic receptor DNA codon molecule and the intended acceptor biomolecule at the other end of the magnetic flux tube. As we will argue below, a similar analysis may be possible with any other location for the dark baryonic particle in **any** atom participating in the bridge complex either at the 'receptor' nucleic acid base codon or at the equivalent 'acceptor' biomolecule at either end of the magnetic flux tube bridge. We are not yet prepared to specifically identify the relevant anatomical locations.

We anticipate this will not be an easy model to market because, for one thing, even at the cosmological level, baryonic dark matter is not detectable by its emitted radiation, its presence can only be inferred from gravitational effects on visible matter composed of other baryons, i.e. protons and neutrons and combinations thereof such as non-emitting ordinary atoms (perhaps the remains of post Big Bang nucleosynthesis activity?). The next barrier anticipated is the convenience of having a super-symmetric state at either end of the transmission flux track complex as discussed below, not to mention the presence of dark baryons (induced or otherwise) at human DNA reproductive codon sites. Maybe this speculation fits better as a wannabe science fiction connecting the human race with an undefined intelligent designer, a believer's kind of stuff . . . . Hollywood producers take notes . . . ☺

We are assuming the presence of the DNA dark baryonic particle(s) with a radius below the threshold Schwarzschild values, i.e., micro black holes. The latter preexisting in the brain either before the transfinite cosmic signal or induced by it upon impact. It is important to note that dark matter particles, regardless of their origination, do not normally carry any <u>electric charge</u> and consequently do not interact with ordinary matter via <u>electromagnetic forces</u>. However if these particles can undergo, sustain and maintain even a transient supersymmetric state after induction, they can join together and undergo <u>annihilation</u> interactions with themselves resulting in the emission of observable by-products such as <u>photons</u> and neutrinos traveling at the speed of light directly to an acceptor biomolecule in resonant frequency phase or indirectly across the magnetic flux bridge complex as detailed. Those photons within a relevant mesoscopic resonant frequency range and maintaining coherence at human body temperature are the subject of quantum chromodynamics (QCD) studies in <u>theoretical physics</u>.

QCD is a theory of the <u>strong interaction</u> (<u>color</u> force), i.e., a <u>fundamental force</u> describing the interactions of the <u>quarks</u> and <u>gluons</u> making up baryons/<u>hadrons</u> as studied in the <u>SU(3) Yang-Mills theory</u> of color-charged <u>fermions</u> or quarks. We are suggesting the possibility that likewise, the entangled or otherwise bonded quarks across the quantum 'synapse' complex form a transient magnetic lock equivalent connecting receptor and acceptor and thereby establishing a flux bridge for superconductive electrons traveling from either side of the 'synapse' and do so in a **Confinement** and transactional mode (see Cramer) where the force between participating quarks does not diminish as they are separated. Because this does not involve gluons, it would not take large amounts of energy to separate two participating quarks when the information transfer is completed as e.g., would be the case if it were instead a <u>proton</u> and a <u>neutron</u> forming a strong interaction link when impacted by the relatively weak transfinite cosmic radiation as demonstrated in the high energy hadron collider experiments. This is better illustrated with the simpler hydrogen atom (proton) forming inter-biomolecular chemical bonds after being impacted by the cosmic particle or axion. Having just outlined the possible wavicle carrying relevant human phylogenetic information from transfinity, we need to continue examining further their characteristics and possible interaction with the brain DNA codon receptor site.

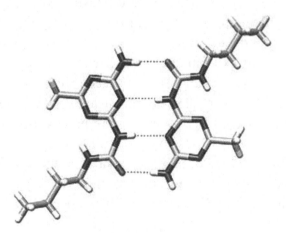

Intermolecular hydrogen bonding.

The transfinite wavicle messenger signal. The unfiltered cosmic particles arriving at the putative brain quantum DNA receptor are composed of almost 90% protons, 9% helium nuclei (alpha particles) and nearly 1% are electrons. It should be of interest that the ratio hydrogen/helium nuclei (28%) present bears the same proportion as that estimated for their primordial elemental abundance ratio (24%). The rest of cosmic radiation is made up of the other Big Bang nucleosynthetic heavier nuclei primarily lithium, beryllium, and boron. The light nuclei appear in much greater abundance (~1%) than in the solar atmosphere, where their abundance is about 10^{-9}% that of helium. In general cosmic radiation comes in two flavors, ionizing and non-ionizing. The former includes Alpha particles, beta particles, gamma rays, X-ray radiation, and neutrons may all carry energies above a few electron volts (ca. 2eV or higher) high enough to ionize target atoms or molecules. Energies >2eV (about 3.2×10^{-19} joules) is enough to match the typical binding energy of an outer valence electron in an atom or organic receptor molecule. This is equivalent to a frequency of ca. 4.8×10^{14} Hz, and a wavelength of 620 nm, e.g., visible red light. Of lesser interest in our mesoscopic energy range brain focus are neutron impacts, the only ones capable of producing radioactive mass (by a process called neutron activation at higher energies) although low speed thermal neutrons carry enough kinetic energy to create unstable isotopes and induce radioactivity without ionizing. It is important to remember that the occurrence of ionization depends almost exclusively on the associated energy of the individual particles or waves, and not on their number.

Of lesser known importance to our analysis is the non-ionizing portion of cosmic radiation consisting mainly of lower energy photon unable to detach electrons from atoms or molecules, i.e., ionizing them, e.g., radio waves, microwaves, infrared and (sometimes) visible light. But why not also consider the elusive **axion particle,** even at the expense of further complicating the architecture of the quantum receptor complex**?**

For instance, what if there may exist, alongside or within the classical baryonic hydrogen atom, a condensed dark counterpart (BEC condensate?) as an isomorphic hybrid or in a 'super-partnership' coupling of sorts? The putative invisible axion, devoid of charges, must consequently depend on **spin** and/or **gravitons** or resonant coupling/entanglement to join an ordinary hydrogen atom instead. However, this shouldn't rule out possible **parallel** chemical exchanges between equivalent axion particles in receptor and/or acceptor sites also. The axion presence in the new DNA dark baryonic atom **receptor** (pre-formed or induced) should not hinder its participation in ordinary physico-chemical exchanges, bonding, etc. with other **acceptor** biomolecules, e.g., during DNA transcription processes.

However, for analytical convenience, we will focus now on the intermolecular gravitational attraction between adjacent dark baryonic hydrogen atoms, **ideally** arranged in a super symmetric, coherent quantum coupling arrangement (superposition), like in a lattice that allows for the superconductivity of those surface electrons displaced by the impacting ionizing radiation and now located in a conduction band to move along the magnetic flux bond(s) formed in the complex.

*It should be mentioned at this point that we are considering the input and output ends of the quantum flux tube complex as forming a <u>magnetic dipole</u> but, because they function independently from each other, both ends may be considered as magnetic monopole <u>quasiparticles</u>. Likewise, e.g., an electron, the hydrogen atom (proton) and <u>subatomic particles</u> have tiny magnetic fields (Dirac strings) and are thereby magnetic monopoles. The degree of alignment of these particle aggregates, sua sponte or induced, determines the strength ρ_m, of the resulting <u>magnetic field</u>, however transient in duration. We are ignoring for convenience the accompanying 'magnetic current density' variable $\mathbf{j}_m$ that results from this controversial Dirac quantization model. Do magnetic particles (gravitons) exist? Why not! Why removing the world-line from space-time? If we include gravity in our mesoscopic level analysis we need to identify the source in the dark baryonic particles below the Schwartschild radius (<u>Planck mass</u>) as we have done. Variations in this limiting radius can be controlled by the levels of <u>Hawking radiation</u> decay when exceeded. Maybe Dirac strings stretch out linking monopoles and those of opposite magnetic charge within range, without disturbing those that hypothetically reaches out to infinity . . . and back! Maybe an updated Maxwell's equation should reflect the self-evident dynamic asymmetry of existential reality we all witness.

*Another possibility is information transfer by 'quantum tunneling' electrons through a <u>barrier</u> that <u>classically</u> they couldn't have surmounted, by creating a *<u>Tunnel junction</u>* by separating two conductors with a very thin insulator. These <u>Josephson junctions</u> take advantage of quantum tunneling and the superconductivity of some <u>semiconductors</u> to create the <u>Josephson effect</u>. It is possible for spin zero particles to travel faster than c when tunneling. The Josephson effect is the phenomenon of 'supercurrent' that flows indefinitely long, without any voltage applied, across two <u>superconductors</u> coupled by a weak link. A Josephson junction can act as a perfect voltage-to-frequency converter. In theory this opens the interesting possibility of a neuronal membrane resting voltage acting as a frequency modulator (FM) of incoming signals.

This will allow for the instantaneous transactional information transfer over long distances between the transfinite source and the brain DNA quantum receptors. The quantum possibility of 'objects' being simultaneously in more than one state makes it possible for DNA to act as a quantum computer **re-transmitting** human phylogenetic information across transfinity.

Ionizing cosmic particle impact on brain DNA baryonic codons. It is not clear whether the dark baryonic state of the brain DNA receptor preceded the cosmic impact or was transiently induced by the transfinite radiation intensity after being filtered by the earth's atmosphere and traveling through human skull bone. In theory the cosmic particle impact may induce the formation of new elements by the process of <u>spallation</u> when the collision causes the expulsion of protons and neutrons from the impacted atomic or molecular DNA codon or biomolecule, e.g., carboxyl groups or any **electronegative** atom like C, N, O in nucleic acids. This has been demonstrated in the upper earth atmosphere. How much reaches earth surface, if any, is an unknown variable.

If the brain DNA dark baryonic state is not induced by the transfinite cosmic/axion radiation then it would be of particular interest to examine the case of cosmic impacts on pre-existing electronegative dark baryonic matter in DNA codons. The possible excitation of their condensed matter upon radiation impacts, forming 'excitons' quasi-particles which can transfer the transfinite source energy without transporting net electric charge. In an electronegative atom an incomplete valence orbital and the impact-displaced electron are attracted to each other (across intramolecular or intermolecular attraction) by an electrostatic Coulomb force yet it is an electrically neutral quasiparticle that can be found in insulators, semiconductors and some liquids. This way the **exciton** is a bound state of an electron and hole which are attracted to each other by the electrostatic Coulomb force providing a stabilizing energy balance. These paradoxical 'bound but free' electrons can exist with their spins in parallel or anti-parallel orientation but can be aligned by a magnetic field or made to flow at superconductive speeds. This has been observed when a cosmic particle is absorbed after impacting matter with a pre-existing (or induced?) semiconductor, lattice arrangement. It is very difficult, but not impossible, to imagine such lattice architecture as formed by hydrogen bonds in structured-water networks at body temperature, e.g., neuron cytoskeleton in the Penrose-Hameroff* model of consciousness. This way, the free electrons originating from the valence band flow into the conduction band and, under the influence of magnetic fields (like those formed in a magnetic flux tube formed by hydrogen bonding), they form a superconductive bridge. The electron spins become coupled by the exchange interaction, giving rise to the exciton fine structure. In such periodic lattices, if demonstrated, the properties of excitons may show momentum (k-vector) dependence.

Magnetic vector field

The magnetic flux bridge formation. Consequent to the cosmic particle (or equivalent radiation) impact on brain DNA receptor matter a hydrogen bond is formed between the proton of a hydrogen atom belonging to either an electronegative nitrogen, oxygen or fluorine of the DNA purine/pyrimidine bases and/or the equivalent atoms from another (or same) molecule or chemical group. The hydrogen atom in the bond must itself be covalently bonded to another electronegative atom in the biomolecule to create the intermolecular bond. The intermolecular hydrogen bond (5 to 30 kJ/mole) is stronger than a van der Waals interaction, but weaker than intra-molecular <u>covalent</u> or <u>ionic bonds</u>. This type of intermolecular bond occurs in both inorganic molecules such as water and <u>organic molecules</u> such as DNA.

The most controversial aspect of this suggested hydrogen bond lattice complex sub-model is the assumption of a fluctuating/dynamic **super**-symmetric hydrogen state, however transient. A **plain** symmetric hydrogen bond is found when the hydrogen proton nucleus is spaced exactly halfway between two other **identical** atoms when the gravitational attraction of the hydrogen atom to each of those other atoms is equal. In the case of the <u>3-center 4-electron bond</u> the strength is much larger than "normal" hydrogen bonds (bond order of 0.5). This magnitude is comparable to a covalent bond. But in <u>particle physics</u>, **supersymmetry** (often abbreviated SUSY) is a more complete <u>symmetry</u> that relates and brings together <u>elementary particles</u> of one <u>spin</u> to other particles that differ by half a unit of spin forming what is known as <u>superpartners</u>. In a type of <u>unbroken</u> supersymmetry we find, in addition, that for every type of <u>boson</u> there exists a corresponding type of <u>fermion</u> with the same mass and internal quantum numbers, and vice-versa. We will see below how hydrogen electrons, a ½ spin **fermionic** particle becomes, upon spin coupling to its equivalent, a **boson** of spin 1,0 particle. To complicate matters further, in our mesoscopic dimension of interest, in order to describe the 4-d Minkowskian low-energy world, one should identify mechanisms that either maintain supersymmetry or disturb it without generating any cosmological constant. It is very complex dealing with <u>supersymmetric theories</u> involving axions because they have both a scalar and a fermionic <u>superpartner</u> all bundled up in a <u>chiral superfield</u>.

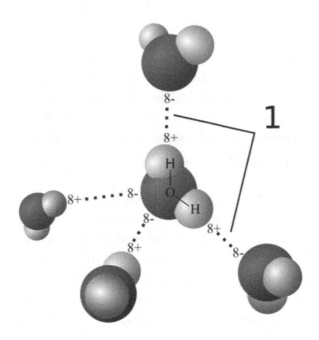

hydrogen bond **donor**   hydrogen bond **acceptor**   hydrogen bond **acceptor**   hydrogen bond **donor**

hydrogen bond **acceptor**

hydrogen bond **acceptor** and/or **donor**

prozac

hydrogen bond **acceptor**

To continue on with the speculation, the possible three co-linear adjacent supersymmetric hydrogen atoms forming the bond may transiently join together as 'superpartners' (forming e.g., the 3 center 4-electron bond) and thereafter stabilize by annihilation liberating photon information energy to a secondary brain acceptor (neocortical neuron membrane?) before the slower classic neuron synaptic complementary/supplementary aspects of the information arrives and converges at the same processing loci.

It is also presumed that ALL relevant (bonded) condensed dark baryon matter somehow function like an integrated semiconductor lattice complex which, upon absorbing a photon of energy from an external (transfinity) or internal (brain) source, forms 'excitons'. If the excitation decays as the displaced electron returns back across the dielectric medium equivalent of such semiconductor arrangement, the EM radiation emitted is called the Cherenkov radiation and we hope it can somehow be detected directly or indirectly. But if not, it travels across the quantum receptor complex to an acceptor and thereby transfers information energy sans the charge component at the speed of light.

But superconductors require electrons to be present in BEC condensates yet loosely bound in <u>Cooper pairs</u> forming lattice semiconductor arrangements where axions are equilibrated with photons under the influence of the magnetic field. Repeating, these electrons with ½ spin and negative charge (i.e., fermions) join positive lattice ions (phonon holes) anywhere in the quantum receptor lattice complex causing electrons to aggregate by exchanging spins among themselves and thereby becoming spin 1,0 electron particles (bosons) easier to transfer information instantaneously at the speed of light as mentioned above. Wikipedia's account of this mechanism is: "The Higgs mechanism occurs whenever a charged field has a vacuum expectation value. In the non-relativistic context, this is the Landau model of a charged Bose-Einstein condensate, also known as a superconductor. In the relativistic condensate, the condensate is a scalar field, and a relativistic invariant. In an actual superconductor, the charged particles are electrons, which are fermions not bosons. So in order to have superconductivity, the electrons need to somehow bind into <u>Cooper pairs</u>. The charge of the condensate q is therefore twice the electron charge e. The pairing in a normal superconductor is due to lattice vibrations, and is in fact very weak; this means that the pairs are very loosely bound. The description of a Bose-Einstein condensate of loosely bound pairs is actually more difficult than the description of a condensate of elementary particles. Axions are predicted to change to and from <u>photons</u> in the presence of strong magnetic fields, and this property is used for creating experiments to detect axions."

The required superconductive state for the reciprocal energy/information transfer in a quantum transaction, as explained above, is accomplished by removing surface electrons from a putative receptor valence position (bound electrons in 'excitons' exhibit a smaller <u>binding energy</u>) into a superconductive mode for transfer to another positively charged 'hole' in an acceptor site, wherever accessible, like the one formed by a previous receptor site, if present. Repeating, as the charged particles travel through they polarize the molecules of that lattice complex medium, which then, if they return back rapidly to their ground state, will emit Cherenkov radiation in the process.

All that remains now in this daring overview is to synthesize all things being considered into a working model with most of the relevant features we have sketched for dark baryonic and dark hydrogen atoms to provide both a Boolean analog and a quantum digital processor when organized as a brain neuronal network at body temperature that will transfer relevant information from transfinity across our suggested quantum receptor architecture complex just like it has been hypothesized for quantum computation information processing when chloroplasts in green plants are similarly impacted by sunlight radiation during photosynthesis, an impressive evidence of quantum coherence in a living system at ambient temperatures as described by the University of Berkeley investigators.

Symmetrical hydrogen bonding

SUMMARY AND CONCLUSIONS

Quantum Receptor Architecture. The final structure/function of this quantum receptor complex must, above all, sustain quantum coherence at human body (brain) temperature, become accessible to measurable attempts at corroboration and become capable of falsifiable predictions. Being part and parcel of a more general biopsychosocial (BPS) neurophilosophical model of consciousness, it should harmonize with the model's foundations on variations on a **transactional interpretation of quantum mechanics** (**TIQM**) describing quantum interactions in terms of a standing wave formed by retarded (forward-in-time) and advanced (backward-in-time) waves as explained in our Volume II. The original model was first proposed in 1986 by John G. Cramer.

Our BPS model, being an 'epistemontological hybrid approach, endorses the 'anthropic principle' and the emphasis on the mesoscopic level of laboratory and philosophical research. This should not be construed as discouraging whatever metaphysical physico-mathematical poem that opens new avenues for creative speculations. This sub-model on a 'quantum receptor complex' is an example. This is illustrated by our implied emphasis on a parallel computing approach in suggesting the presence of multiple processing elements simultaneously present in the quantum receptor complex to solve the problem of reciprocal transactional information transfer between man and that transfinity something that somehow guides and inspires our species to transcend the subhuman condition in conceptually building an ordered cosmos that defies the entropy laws of nature.

In a nutshell, electromagnetic and gravitational (read the quantum vs. relativistic) realities suggests independent pathways to solve the same problem of existential reality for the human species without the necessary violation of the combined symmetries of <u>charge conjugation</u> and <u>parity</u>, We are trying to bring all the known ontological/epistemological approaches by breaking the problem into independent parts so that each processing element can execute its part of the quantum receptor algorithm simultaneously with the others. The processing elements present in the quantum receptor complex can be diverse but are synthesized to include all analytical resources in a single brain combinatorial computer with multiple processor elements, the perceptual, the conceptual, or any substantiated privileged ESP communication, e.g., 'revelation' or any combination of the above.

** Coming now to specifics, supposing we were to bring together all of these dark baryonic hydrogen atoms together into a functional lattice network complex as that described for structured water molecular dipoles found in 70% of brain substance constituting a quantum field. Frohlich has described how quantum coherent waves states can be generated by neuronal biomolecules and propagated along a neuronal network. It is believed that this activity is responsible for the gamma wave synchronization in the EEG. As mentioned above, many quanta may condense (BEC) into a single state allowing long range synchronizing correlations between the dipoles. Water molecules with a high electric dipole moment have been demonstrated to have periodic oscillations.

In closing, one wonders how much of the brain biophysical chemistry can account for the dynamics of a self conscious mind in the wakeful state. Can a quantum receptor complex, as explained, adequately link or interface the unfathomable quantum vacuum continuum with the human conscious effort to explain it to itself and others? Is that enough? Is the intercalation of an invisibility like **dark** matter adequate to throw **light** into the epistemontological conundrum of mind—body interactions, i.e., is the mind physical, as explained, but invisible? Last, but not least, may this speculation on the participation of reproductive gene sites (DNA dark baryonic codons) open a new chapter in human <u>evolutionary biology</u> linking the fitness landscapes or adaptive biopsychosocial landscapes to unknown metaphysiological elements in the dark chemistry of <u>genotypes</u> giving rise to de novo human brain special behavioral <u>phenotypes</u> explaining both its unusual <u>reproductive success</u> when compared to other species and its spectacular <u>flawed forms</u> as expressed in their animals-like reactions to <u>supernormal stimuli</u> as witnessed in armed war conflicts.

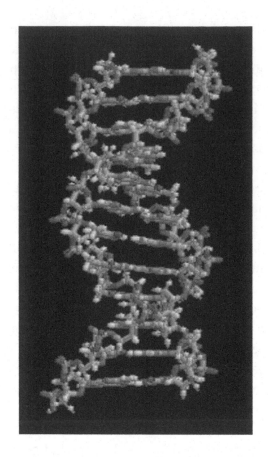

Dr. Angell O. de la Sierra, Esq. In Deltona, Florida Winter 2010
http://angelldls.wordpress.com/

* * *

Lux, Veritas et Vitae

ABSTRACT

How do we humans make decisions? Are they rooted on 'beliefs' or reason? What are, or should be, the principles on which all of our ordinary judgments be based? Are we free to make decisions? These are some of the questions we will consider when attempting to identify the possible source(s) of righteousness.

INTRODUCTION

We intend to develop further previous incursions into the conscious processes underlying the search for meanings associated with unfamiliar environmental stimuli previously processed at subconscious levels. In so doing we will stress the importance of a rational, self conscious agency operating by seeking to be the first cause of its subsequent deliberative actions with the assistance of the language faculty. By subjecting the novelty experienced to a conscious a-priori analytical dissection followed by an a-priori synthetic dissection on its specifics we may arrive at a synthetic a-posteriori conclusion to guide the continuing search for the best adaptive solution to choose from pre-existing and available probable alternatives, what we have called 'free will by consent'. We will highlight the interplay between beliefs and reasons and how we should strive to clearly identify the 'thing' we consciously will to produce or bring about, i.e., an end, as an adaptive solution to our immediate problem and to the world whenever/wherever the same problem may come up. This way 'the end' will guide my actions into deliberations about means of producing that result. Once I have adopted an end in this sense, it dictates that I do something about it and ideally I will act in ways that will bring about that 'end' according to first humanity principles. How so?

Our neuro-philosophy model of consciousness, following biopsychosocial (BPS) preservation guidelines, dictates what **not** to do (other possibly interfering things) so I am able to execute my choice plan. This way, the free will of every conscious rational being becomes *a will that either argues for, or follows universal laws.* Arguably our fundamental moral obligation is to act only on principles which could earn acceptance by a community of fully rational agents each of whom have an equal share in arguing in behalf of these principles for their community or state. These arguments, a post-Kantian extension of his "categorical imperatives", represent goals to be nurtured when humanity, not the individual, is in search of proper responses to its real time existential problems. As such, it is an *objective* end, because it is an end that every rational being must have insofar as the individual is rational. Consequently, it should limit what I am *morally permitted* to do when I pursue my selfish *and* subjective negative ends . . . . , as a goal. Many complex problems arise when we try to force the equality beliefs = reason = natural laws = universal laws. What is the difference?

ARGUMENTATION

Do we innately distinguish the self interest from that of others (humanity)? When we do, humanity in oneself is the source of a duty to develop one's talents or to 'perfect' one's humanity. Or better, to encourage the humanity of others as when recognizing values that have met some standard of evaluation appropriate to persons. What comes first? Ideally there should be no conflict because true freedom does not imply being bound by no law, but by self-imposed 'laws' that are in some sense of one's own rational/moral making. True autonomy, when individually applied, should ensure that the source of the authority of the moral law principles that binds self is one's own rational will, i.e., one that operates in response to reasons, free from physically or psychologically imposed controls such as e.g., slavery, deranged obsessions or other medical thought disorders, etc.

However, it should be noticed a distinction between a will being determined through the operation of natural laws **subconsciously** controlling the biopsychosocial equilibrium and those operating in response to reasons in a normal **conscious** free subject. The subjective conscious belief of being free is established empirically and, as such, cannot be subjected to a rational a-priori analytical scrutiny as an argument to invoke a Kantian Categorical Imperative. Are we 'free' when engaged in quotidian existential endeavors, here and now, trying to decide what to do, what to hold oneself and others responsible for? Can the existential constraints, when observed, still be justified in holding such behavior as conscious and autonomous free wills? If we consider the human species existence as a neo-Copernican reality and take into account the self evident fact of our species sensory and brain combinatorial limitations, it would not be as difficult to conceive of a compromise between pure and practical reason as Kant tried without much success when he introduced the muddled synthetic a-priori argumentation. This, because existential reality, however limited, is in our human brains and consequently humans are at the center of the universe and are the reason for all things, those that are and those that are not. Contrary to metaphysical logic claims, mathematics is a convenient language we humans invented, not discovered, to represent environmental phenomenal sensations, experienced as perceptual brain 'feelings' and represented as symbols or sentences when physically absent or as 'invisibilities' below the threshold of sensory detection. This is the rationale for an epistemontological hybrid conceptual model of real time, existential reality.

It is a foregone conclusion that there is no **rational** basis on which to root any belief that the natural world we experience is (or is not) structured according to some purpose by an intelligent Designer. But, there is also a rational basis on which to logically predict or believe that something, somehow, somewhere has caused the phenomenological structures and/or functions we, our brains, experience. To invoke self creation is living in convenient, sometimes perverse denial because, deny it or not, we are all believers, rational thinking demands it! This does not mean we should not insist on the actual practice of science and technology to look, search and describe for us the phenomenal 'what' and the practical 'how' but also speculate on the purpose of chemicals, cells, tissues, organs, creatures, environments, and so on from the micro to the cosmological levels of organization. And leave the noumenal what and why of the 'design' to metaphysical logic evaluation, when available, that should not exclude the search for answers outside the 4-d space time Minkowsky confinement imposed on our species, reason demands it! If there is a convincing reason, other than self-serving pre-judgments, it should become available for dispassionate analysis. We can use the same argument to concede that, while there is no rational justification for anyone's belief that our conscious and free wills are (or are not) free, the subconscious accessing of higher order explanations are geared to search for the right casual chain that includes the origin, and for the curious (and retired ☺), also a continuing search for the first causes of things. All of this consciously and freely willed, operating according to a universal law, not imposed but one of which I, the individual, am the origin or author!

Yet, please notice that, according to the methodology rules of the game, an **analytic** a-priori scrutiny applies to a **rational** entity. Existential reality requires that the human rational agency must take the means to our individualized empirical ends not methodologically subject to a proper analytic a-priori rational analysis. Thus there seems to be a conflict between the analytic claim characterizing standard philosophy methodology and the supposed **synthetic** conclusion that a **rational** agency also requires when conforming to a further, non-desire based, principle of practical reason such as the Kantian categorical imperative, deontologigal variation, claiming that there is 'something'(?) in the 'rational synthesis' which is an end in itself. In other words, the important thing was for Kant, not the rational solution to the individualized existential problem but instead that a free rational conscious will was the righteous source of moral authority. This *abstract value* was not necessarily related to *value of the **result*** intended in real time existence by the conscious willing. It would seem as if theoreticians often lose sight that they are biopsychosocial beings themselves with all of the existential implications on the priorities that subconsciousness defends and unfortunately only knowledge and good experiences can overcome. This is a fact of life the recorded history of mankind can testify to. Rousseau's "Social Contract" conclusions on the innate good nature of man that the society of men corrupt carries an inherent contradiction. Recorded history makes it credible that only the knowledge and predictable certainty of the **few,** when graced with a good upbringing, superior intelligence and access to possible unconventional revelation sources, can guide their decision-making process. This background for righteousness is uncommon. Inferential knowledge from historical traditions, i.e., as found in scriptural writings, is also relevant and important and may not qualify as rational in the philosophical point of view. Different from 'reason', **beliefs** have two dimensions: a historical point of reference (tradition) and an existential emotionally-laden imperative associated with species survival (BPS equilibrium.) which at times counter each other because constancy of tradition is assumed and the dynamic evolution of BPS equilibrium cannot temporally synchronize.

We also need to distinguish between negligent and intentional behavior patterns beyond what is coded law. Should punishable life-patterns stem from various negligent failures of **reason** imposed by the political system or its total absence as imposed by health related inheritance? In addition we need to look into the question of whether revelation is dependent on traditional sensory input or is it transmitted from another unconventional source, such as God directly or a hypostasized, **created** or living intermediary prophet?

If created as an epistemological model to mediate, what are the rules guiding the model, whose rules, whose reasons could be arrived at independently by any rational human being? In other words, these are 'laws' which ought to 'make sense' to any reasonable person, and, as such, are basic, natural moral laws which, left to our own devices, we ought come up with on our own, e.g., things like prohibitions against murder, adultery, theft, lying and abusing flora and fauna. Can the laws of reason equate with natural laws? Are they grounded on BPS survival considerations? Are they connected as an inseparable epistemontological hybrid? Reason and revelation assist each other. The theologically inspired commandments and prohibitions become the equivalents of the secular ethical laws of nature. Reason alone has it that, with their guidance, man is able to work for a hypothetical salvation, he has earned it.

Intuitively and as Kant suggested, ". . . revelation, tradition and prophecy are all intimately related." This, because revelation, if ever present to some, is supported, if nothing else, by acting in accordance with basic, reason-based moral ideals. Existence is itself an unknown (divine?) gift. Revelation and knowledge-from-tradition are distinct from reason-based knowing and may ultimately be one and the same effort to satisfy the innate drive to explain our existence as to origins and destinations.

The order instituted by God, or an intelligent designer equivalent, whereby everlasting happiness is arguably achieved by man's labors in fulfillment of the self imposed law. God beliefs supplements a secular **natural law ethics** (and/or a 'Virtue Theory' ethics) with a divine command theory for the purpose of increasing human survival potential as a species. Reason, in this way, is helped by revelation. What is natural law ethics? By the life, death and passion of prophets and their prayerful mode of facing them exemplifies that there is a time to give and time to receive . . . . And a probable, unidentified source of righteousness?

SUMMARY AND CONCLUSIONS

Any neurophilosophy model of human consciousness will eventually have to address the important issue of the decision-making process. We have detailed in three previous volumes what we think is at the core of existential human behavior in a real time, 4-dimensional Minkowsky world. We concentrated then on the bottoms up elements that transmit information from our internal (body proper) and 4-d external environment. These included genetic and memetic sources, all in place to guarantee the survival of the species, at least to reproductive age and included biological, psychic and social elements (BPS). This may be considered the subconscious phase strategies for maintaining a BPS equilibrium as in any other subhuman species.

However, when confronted with novel, unfamiliar environmental contingencies / stimuli, programmed solutions in genetic and memory data bases are necessary but insufficient to attain and sustain a biopsychosocial equilibrium and we had to change shift and draw on 'top-down' self conscious strategies to improvise anew adaptive solutions. These included a completion of the analytic a priori scrutiny for content of new stimuli and a summary of the available neuro-humoral and neuromuscular resources for an effective execution of an adaptive response.

We now deal with what goes on between receptor and effector, how do we make decisions in response to new situations, what role do secular ethics and theological moral codes play, i.e., the role logical reason and beliefs play respectively? What are the sources of righteousness? The answers have remained unanswered for centuries. In our brief discussion we draw heavily from Kant and St. Thomas Aquinos in orienting our own epistemontological hybrid approach.

Emmanuel Kant was one of the first serious philosophers to address the principle(s) on which all of our ordinary moral judgments are based when making decisions. Ideally, the judgments in question are supposed to be those any normal, sane, adult human being would accept. Today, we dare question the sufficiency of his overly optimistic 'synthesis a priori' conclusions about the depth and extent of real time existential moral agreement. What is important about his conclusions is that his foundational moral principle is anchored on the requirement that the decision flows from an individual person's own free and rational will. But what about the complexities of quotidian human existence, such as what is revealed in human psychology, social interaction, political and religious passions, etc. How can they be framed as ethical obligations? How may a personal goal fit inside a frame of moral virtuosity and complete happiness by assuming the former is a condition sine qua non for deserving the latter? We posit that a biopsychosocial well being, in equilibrium with existential reality, as argued, is the best probable moral perfection most of us can hope for. A virtuous human life in conflict with self well being is the exception to the abstract, logical and universal moral law that rational thinking brings about when it cannot account for the theological guidance and inspiration for righteousness a **few** historical prophets experienced. But, the transfinite sources of righteousness even for those few need to be **explained** by any means, including faith, not necessarily **described** in its probable unintelligible complexity.

We have questioned in the preceding perambulating ramblings, the methodology that standard moral philosophy employs when evaluating the worth of beliefs and rationality when consciously and freely processing novel, unfamiliar environmental information as part of an integral view of a brain dynamics model when in search of appropriate **meanings** of novel contingencies. The latter precedes any subsequent effort to solve the **particular**, **individualized** problem at hand, as opposed to providing **universal** guidelines applicable to **any** innominate general human contingency in one's existence. Once we identify the fundamental philosophical issues that must be addressed analytically *a priori*, i.e., without drawing on empirical observations of human beings and their behavior, we may then **match** the results with facts drawn from experience in order to determine how best to apply this principle to real time human beings and generate particular conclusions about how we ought to act then, and hopefully anytime a similar issue comes up. Kant's original emphasis on an exclusive *a priori* analytical method to establish fundamental moral principles seems lacking and in contradiction for it is common knowledge that our conscious free will is determined by practical considerations and various motivations, including negative ones, and may produce or not the right actions. Besides, secular ethical codes usually rely on empirical generalizations. A compromise between the logical requirements of an a priori analytical tool and existential reality is necessary.

Since **observation** cannot adequately establish the necessary conformity of rational wills to the Categorical Imperative, Kant cleverly regards the claim that they do conform as an example of an *a priori synthetic* claim, i.e., an *a priori* claim that is not analytic or conceptual because their justification **cannot** rely on observation. This is the questionable reason Kant held fundamental issues in ethics must be addressed with an *a priori* method because the ultimate subject matter of ethics is the nature and content of the principles that necessarily determine a rational will. Is an 'a priori synthetic' method a de facto an 'a posteriori synthetic method? An *a posteriori* method seems ill-suited to discovering and establishing what we *must* do; surely it will only tell us what we *actually* do. For *a posteriori* considerations would thus result in a tainted conception of moral requirements, based on individualized BPS considerations. E.g., the idea of a good will is supposed to be the idea of one who only makes decisions that he holds to be morally worthy, taking moral considerations in themselves to be conclusive reasons for guiding his behavior. This sort of disposition or character is something we all highly value. Kant believes we value it without limitation or qualification. But, good will must then also be good *in itself* and not in virtue of its relationship to other things such as the agent's own happiness or overall welfare.

What follows, as a parting shot, is an afterthought of what may seem like a neuroscientist attempt to navigate the unfamiliar waters of moral philosophy without a lifesaver and a faulty engine. But, one would expect that, before addressing such question as what is a duty to act righteously, one would have to know **who** is responding, under what **circumstances** and to **what** stimulus. Naturally, if one were to choose a 'metaphysics of morals' as a guide to the answer, it would have to be an account of the nature and structure of existential moral reality, a categorization of specific duties and values for specific problems as they arise in real time existence. Metaphysical questions are scrutinized by established *a priori* methods. Conformity to moral requirements has formally nothing to do with a conscious, autonomous rational agency. We have all read newspaper accounts of the immoral behavior of a perfectly rational agent! To say that what is really important is not the subject but his inner principles is an abstraction of questionable social value unless we deny that a man does not exist independent from the very circumstances that make him the man he actually is in reality. Furthermore, is **rational free agency** to feel constrained to act in certain ways that we *might* not want to, or the thought that we have moral duties? A dutiful action from any of these biopsychosocial motives, however praiseworthy it may be, does not necessarily express a good will because assuming an action has moral worth **only** if it expresses a good will, independent of the probable negative consequences, such actions, have no genuine 'moral worth'. Perhaps the motivational structure of a conscious and free rational agent be better arranged on the basis of duty priority under the unavoidable and relevant circumstances surrounding the individualized case, and this includes a consideration of the unavoidable human emotion concomitants. Translated into out brain dynamics model, the motivation should be predicated on the subject's BPS viability. This should not be construed as ignoring the force of abstract moral requirements as reasons because arguably, they retain their reason-giving force under **any** circumstance and ergo, they have universal validity. In what universe free of conditions or circumstances, one may ask? Does it make sense that because of being ill informed, negligent or outright intentional in having antecedently adopted some conflicting goal for ourselves, we should be considered rational enough to understand the complex, the obscure, the unexpected, the unintelligible and act on it, simply because we possess a conscious and rational free will? This is an appeal for more conceptual development of hypothetical imperatives as a realistic conditional force, taking into account emotional and cognitive states the subject may or may not be in and in virtue of his conscious free *desiring* or *wanting,* an end compatible with real time, ongoing biopsychosocial equilibrium and well being which Kant himself recognized as "natural necessities . . . and practical law". Even then, there is no guarantee that "the ends we will, we might not have willed, and some ends that we do not will we might nevertheless have willed". Conscious, rational free agents will the **necessary and available** means to any ends that they will, what Aquinos called "practical rationality". This way we are committed, albeit imperfectly, to the care and sustenance of our niche in the biosphere ecosystem, as the intelligent designer somewhere in transfinity cares for the entire universe.

We argue that the precepts of the natural laws direct us toward the universal good as well as various particular goods and thus provide the pure and practical reasons for us conscious rational beings to be aware and act pursuant to their benefits. We urge the appropriate professionals to transform this implicit awareness into explicit and propositional legislation free from strong emotions or evil dispositions. Natural law is that good is to be done and evil avoided, good is the pursuit of a healthy, happy and socially convivial life as implied in the biopsychosocial equilibrium (BPS) state.

But how is universal, natural goodness possible? For one might hold, as Aquinos did, ". . . that human beings' common nature, their similarity in physiological constitution, makes them such as to have some desires in common, and these desires may be so central to human aims and purposes that we can build important and correct precepts of rationality around them". For something to be good is not that it stands in some relation to desire but rather that it is somehow "*perfective* or *completing*" of a being, where what is perfective or completing of a being depends on that being's nature. The most appropriate response an existing real time conscious and free human to the goods available cannot be **absolutely** determined by any master legislation or philosophical method, but can be determined only by the involvement of the JudeoChrIslamic theological institutions or their equivalent secular appeal to the insight of the conscious rational and autonomous persons of genuine practical wisdom, the rightness of actions in rational agency, itself a moral value as argued. When we stress from the pulpit, the temple or the mosque the importance of that collection of features that make us distinctively human, and these include capacities to engage in self-directed rational behavior, and thereby adopt and pursue our own reasonable ends, and any other capacities necessarily connected with these, then we are truly free.

Dr. Angell O. de la Sierra, Esq. In Deltona, Florida Spring 2012

REFERENCES

1. http://plato.stanford.edu/entries/kant-moral/
2. Timmerman, Jens, 2007, *Kant's Groundwork for the Metaphysics of Morals: A Commentary*. New York: Cambridge University Press.
3. http://plato.stanford.edu/entries/moral-epistemology/#Bib
4. http://angelldls.wordpress.com/

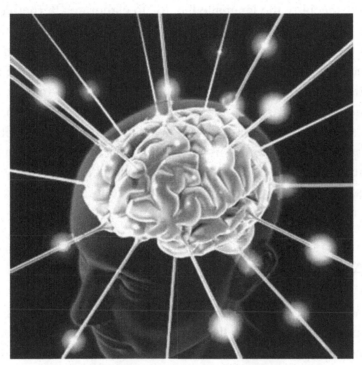

Reciprocal, Transactional Information Transfer

INTRODUCTION

Just what is the **evidence** for a <u>physical,</u> functional <u>mind</u>? Invisible entities require indirect but consistent evidence of their physical existence, unless we conclude it has no independent existence and, like colors, depends on a visible substrate brain. Unlike in colors, brain substrates require to be living and introspectibly accessible by the beholder to give testimony of its existence as the embodiment of the conscious state. No brain, no mind. But what are the distinctive functional properties of the conscious state of self and others? A thermostat can be **aware** of subtle changes in ambient temperature and be programmed to respond in precise ways without itself being aware of its own identity and that of others. This is probably the situation of most subhuman species and intelligent robots. What is our **conscious** relation to self and others? We need to be able to represent others first <u>perceptually</u> as sense-phenomenal objects or events and then, with the assistance of memory, <u>conceptually</u> as thoughts or beliefs of their physical existence in their absence. These correspond to first order and second order representations respectively. The phenomenal awareness of the thermostat, as electronically reported, lacked the subjective dimension that has 'feel', or *that* it is *like something* to experience, as linguistically reported (or not) during consciousness. When the perceptual reality becomes familiar and presents no threats to the species biopsychosocial (BPS) integrity or equilibrium we develop reflex responses to their subsequent presence and need only to become aware of their ongoing physical or memory presence, not necessarily conscious. When the perceptual or conceptual presence is unfamiliar, we need to find meanings absent from their first and second order representations. We need to access the brain consumer faculties, especially the language faculty, to elaborate alternatives of responses (if any needed) in the form of third order symbolic or sentential representations based on our native language as the basis on which to apply rational logic principles on the one hand and ethical/moral learned standards on the other hand. We briefly discuss the neuro-anatomical substrates of emotions and how they may influence the decision-making process we posit to be enacted at the cortical attractor phase space of the brain pre-motor area. Finally we speculate on the possible neuronal networks involved in reciprocal transactional information transfer between brain and transfinity as an explanation of possible sources of righteous guidance and inspiration for those historical prophets who under adversity, in the absence of organized religions, were able to perform altruistic acts contrary to nature and self interest in observance of universal laws of ethics and moral behavior.

ARGUMENTATION

Most objective and dedicated neuroscientists, philosophers, engineers, mathematicians, theologians or psychiatrists will agree that either the human mind is embodied in the brain or somehow depends on it for its existential functionality. Yet, as Ramon y Cajal early on experienced, a biopsy of any deep or superficial brain tissue would immediately reveal the incompleteness and insufficiency of the redundant, ubiquitous neuronal sameness, that which to the naïve investigator seems necessary and sufficient at first sight. The most elementary understanding of the 'mind' requires an interdisciplinary approach and a neutral open mind to accept the immanent and the transcendental, the perceptual sensory facts and the conceptual inferences, the invisible micro and the cosmological macro, the intuitions and revelations, the physical and metaphysical. This we call a physical grasp of a functional mind.

To begin understanding the mind you need first to understand how is the human brain organized, structurally and functionally. Like in most advanced subhuman species the brain responds in a stereotypical way to internal (body proper) and external environmental threshold stimulation that posit a potential threat to the biological integrity of the organism. The stereotypical reflex response to sensory stimulation involves the activation of genetically inherited, neuron-coded archetypes which adaptively avoid or repel the offending stimulant at unconscious levels with the prominent participation of the brain's amygdaloidal body. It is presumed that, as part of the protective scanning process inherited, we also acquire by learning the ability to code for, and store in memory, equivalent neuronal network archetypes by associating the stimulus with the particular environmental *context* previously registered in memory as dangerous, thus adding a new subconscious dimension to the processing. The hippocampus complex plays a significant role in providing the memory recall of the *context* in which the object/event sensed was considered dangerous. This is usually termed the subconsciously-activated, acquired/learned, memetic component to distinguish it from the unconsciously-activated, inherited/genetic component. The latter is termed a *first order* account/representation which may be modified (complemented/supplemented) by memories and stored as *second order* representations now available (hippocampus complex) for further conscious, *third order* representation-processing if needed.

Sense-phenomenal accounts (or their non-phenomenal thought/feeling equivalents) in the form of original memory experiences can be further modified depending on the neuro-hormonal activation induced at any relevant stage of the modification. This adds an additional emotional layer which will play a significant influence also at later stages in the decision-making process. It is fair to assume that first order genetic, hard wired archetype representations are unconsciously recalled to preserve the biological integrity of the species and existed long before the brain's thalamo-cingulate gyrus was able to elaborate emotions in response to neuro-humoral system co-participation. It is important to remember that the unconscious amygdaloid avoidance response to a sensory object/event can be elicited long before such object/event was possibly witnessed by the subject and consequently this first order representation lacks emotions associated with pleasurable mental well being or social acceptance. This does not imply that previous Lysenko-type environmental coding may get incorporated into the genetic code for further propagation. How? Quare.

However, as the newborn sensory system develops, especially the amygdaloidal-cingulate gyrus projections, a second order representation becomes possible. Now a context analysis becomes another protective layer differentiation between, e.g., the lion behind the zoo cage bars as distinguished from one freely roaming in a jungle setting! Now body postures, facial expressions, sounds and sightings add a new dimension to the protective reflex activity operating at subconscious levels of integration. As the neocortex development continues past toddler age, a new, most important layer of protection, beyond the subconscious second order representation, becomes available as soon as an introspective self analysis is able to discover that 'I' am the subject experiencing that jungle sight, hearing that roaring sound. If the experience is familiar and safe, according to genetic and memetic data base comparisons, there is no need for further processing; as when driving through my rough neighborhood while texting a message! If unfamiliar, e.g., lions escaped the zoo and roam the neighborhood streets, the amygdaloid first and hippocampus second order representations are necessary to activate the avoidance reflex and fight/flight response but not sufficient to guarantee the psychic and social equilibrium beyond the biological safeguards. Emotions run high because it's me in fear. The sense phenomenal pathways are all activated, including both the thalamic-alert reticular activating system (RAS) and the thalamic gates connection to the matured cingulate gyrus where emotional feelings are stored and ready to be mobilized by the central hypothalamus and peripheral (sympathetic/parasympathetic) autonomic system as part of a coordinated Cannon response that includes hormonal activation, e.g., suprarenal gland. Any adaptive response to an unfamiliar novelty can be the result of immanent unconscious or subconscious reflex activity, as discussed, but it would be incomplete until we analyze the contextual meaning of that novel object, event or thought, we need to access whatever consumer neuronal networks are available in the brain (or elsewhere?), e.g., the language faculty and the third order representations therein available. Can its rational analysis efficaciously interfere and influence preceding and subsequent **reflex** activity? Can emotions trump the **rational** activity? The answer to both questions is yes and it depends on the individual and his existential circumstances, all because of that uniquely human species attribute we call conscious free will.

Both these levels of protective, automatic processing can be interfered with by a self-conscious will to act against self interest as will be discussed below for altruistic behaviors. In other words, the next level of sensory input processing deals with the search for meaning of unfamiliar/novel objects/events experiences, all in anticipation of an adequate adaptive response. This brings into play the role language, free will, cognition and emotions have in the decision-making process and the associated brain geographies most likely participating. That is to say, stereotyped reflex behaviors, inherited or learned, are hardwired and normally not subject to volitional control by the subject, except as noted. The acquired elements constitute the conditioned movement patterns that arise in learning processes. The conscious processes will eventually identify the probabilities of adaptive success of action targets and goals preceding volitional behaviors subsequently to be executed by the patterned generation and mobilization of neuromuscular activity in cortical pre-motor neuron pools.

We need to stay focused on what we mean when we say we are 'conscious', it means only that we are in a state of mind where introspectively we can differentiate between the novel object/event being experienced at that instant and ourselves as the subject or observer, i.e., a self conscious state. Only then can we begin the search for 'what' that experience means to ME, my health, my mental well being or my social relationship with others, for what we have reserved the term biopsychosocial equilibrium or BPS equilibrium for short. For reasons that we have analyzed and detailed elsewhere, we have singled out this precise moment as a very probable instant where thought and language are co-generated to participate in the elaboration of a dynamic (editable) mindscape where perceptual and conceptual aspects are integrated as the unit basis for a probable final rational response. The final stage in the decision-making process is related to 'how' we feel emotionally with that choice as compared to competing adaptive solutions. Which one can 'I' freely consent to and be happy with the short and long term consequences?

Interestingly, one can see the rational mind, in its axiologic quest for universal principles, as being continuously challenged by existential, neuro-humoral-assisted, individualized emotional demands for human biopsychosocial survival in a real space-time world of impending dangers and species competition. Yet, survival of the human species ultimately requires one common source of righteousness encompassing the virtues of Lux, Veritas et Vitae. One may properly ask, what is the ideal combination of these competing survival imperatives? What is more important in shaping the proper human personality, the inherited or the learned, is there a third alternative? Should BPS circumstances or theological revelations guide our existential behavior? After all, we cannot deny that emotional memories, when integrated into cognition, will chisel out much of the configuration of our personal universal values. Yet history has recorded the lives of prophets living before the existence of organized religions that have withstood the embattled stresses of existence, have ignored negative emotional influences when making decisions and instead opted for the free conscious choice of universal values as found—or not—in secular codes of ethics and theological scripts of moral behavior. What or where was their source of guidance and inspiration? How did it happened, and why? Ultimately, is it all about our individualized existential survival or the idealized collective survival of the species? Is that the equivalent of a living BPS equilibrium or the idealized goal, respectively?

One may conveniently conceptualize life, physicalist's style, as a reflective reflex experience. Reflex because the Sherrington elements adequately explain most of our lifetime experiences, not very different from other advanced subhuman species. The afferent arm of the reflex elements range, from the bottoms up, internal, external and propio-receptors, connecting inter-neurons, thalamic relays, alert stations and a sensory cortex. From the topside down we complete the reflex arc by processing the sensory input and transferring the results to pre-motor cortex to control the motor cortex neuron pool in the selection of the adaptive efferent motor neurons to activate the smooth or skeletal musculature or gland into an effector response. As noted, this reflex control involves genetic and memory neuronal archetype activation.

In the absence of significant neuro-humoral, body proper or external environmental sensory inputs the brain depends on memory recalls to sustain at least a state of subconscious awareness, if not self consciousness, before the subject lapses into sleep. This sleep state should not be construed as an incapacity for continued memory storage, as illustrated when we recall REM dreams. The brain also spends considerable energy processing working memories into more permanent forms for retrieval access, comparing them to previous records and modifying the details of the appropriate sensory modality when needed.

This second order level does not include either the volitional conscious behavior or the brain's language faculty participation. The pre-conscious level is originated and sustained instead by both pre-programmed hard wired reflexes (controlled along the neuraxis spinal cord, brainstem, etc.) of genetic origin and learned/acquired conditioned reflexes.

However, according to the dynamic BPS model, conscious free will can significantly influence and efficiently suppress these types of reflex behaviors in response to exigent circumstances inspired by self BPS equilibrium preservation or contrariwise, even against self interest in altruistic situations. We can demonstrate how athletes can learn to modify their previous hard wired neuromuscular patterns of movement by consciously willing the new modification results. This claim obviously brings yet another dimension of species preservation that escapes the certainty grasp of scientific methodology and metaphysical logic apprehension. It is precisely the self-evident activity of being able to consciously control nature's genetically imposed reflex behavior patterns at will that forces a metaphysical logic complementation to the measured results from scientific methodology. Because of the well known limitations in the sensory and computational resolution capacity of the human brain a hybrid conceptual approach is imposed to integrate the physical ontological with the metaphysical epistemological, the perceptual with the conceptual, i.e., an epistemontological BPS model. Of course we also have the choice of a self-imposed view of existential reality by limiting ourselves to exclusively consider the measurable, falsifiable aspects of reality. But we can also consciously choose to remove the physical blinders and gamble on the open-ended probability calculus predictions offered by quantum theory instead of the assumed certainty of the perceptually obvious and ignoring everything else relevant but outside the direct or instrument-aided observation threshold. This approach requires a flexible, multidisciplinary attitude. That means a willingness to occasionally serve time inside that frustrating cyclic prison of speculations going nowhere, or going to positive or negative infinities, etc. Dark matter baryons, God's particles, brainßàtransfinity reciprocal, transactional information transfer, intelligent design, etc. are but a few examples of theoretical platitudes. But before we fly we need to crawl and then walk through the quick sand of unfamiliar disciplines to learn about the physical brain and the metaphysical mind and how they are related to the living and the self conscious state. Before we navigate from the unconscious and subconscious manifolds briefly outlined above, we need to get more familiar with the physical brain substrate where the seemingly metaphysical mind is embodied in terms of higher order neural network representations. Is this enough? We think not until we develop and incorporate the probability of reciprocal transactional information transfer between human neocortex and transfinity in an effort to better understand the source of righteousness and the intelligent design that theologians and prophets have sketched in human recorded history.

Our wakeful life in a familiar environment is characterized by and large by learned responses to known objects or events that require our immediate or delayed attention and disposition. With the exception of olfaction, most other sensory information input arriving from receptors have a synaptic relay station at the thalamus before proceeding to the sensory alerted cortex as noted above. Once being subjected to a comparison analysis with memory sensory data, if novel, it gets stored for future use while the search for meaning continues before a response is executed if needed. In very general terms, information input into memory reservoirs is controlled by NMDA synaptic receptors which, upon depolarization and long term potentiation, substitute receptor channel Mg^{++} for Ca^{++} that now flows and finds its way into the synaptic cytosol. Its presence triggers the genetic expression of required synaptic proteins. If sensory input is recognized as safe and familiar, reflex connections to cortical premotor area will subconsciously unleash the appropriate learned effector responses retrieved from memory storage.

The search for an adaptive response starts at the previously reticular-activated primary sensory cortex and travels to hippocampus and cingular cortex. From first person reports and measurements the most retrievable memories are usually experiences associated with both high-emotional content and duration, especially if the memory has been reinforced by previous deliberate or accidental recalls. Measurements include EEG, MEG, fMRI, ERP (Event-Related-Potentials) and local electrode recordings of thalamo-cortical reciprocal synchronization of information exchanges. This exchange between thalamic intralaminar nuclei and superficial pyramidal cell dendrites generating the elusive beta waves is most interesting in that it provides fidelity of information transfer from thalamic relays across all cortex layers. What is more significant to us is the association of the object or event with meaningful cognitive inferences within the context of the subject's BPS circumstance which makes it more accessible for retrieval.

Sometimes, for didactic purposes, one can simplify complexity for the purpose of orientation. One may conceptualize a living brain as operating at two different wakeful cognitive states: awareness and self-conscioussness. As noted earlier, **awareness** depends on genetic/memory sensory input and stereotyped, involuntary motor output forming a reflex loop of varying degrees of involuntary motor sophistication and operating at non-conscious levels of activity as they may be generated from the wakeful or sleep states. The **self-conscious** subject, on the other hand, can go beyond the genetic and memory repertoire of resources and consciously improvise new solutions for similar or novel contingencies of the perceptual or conceptual variety arising from internal or external environment stimuli. Another additional exclusive feature of the self-conscious state is that it can amplify weak stimulations and select which of several sensory/abstract events to concentrate on and in what sequence. Only the self-conscious state can willfully rehearse and parade previous relevant scenarios stored in cortical attractor phase spaces for comparison, modification or actual adoption as the final choice response. Memory recalls and sensory hyper-stimulation initiate, reinforce and sustain the awakened state, self conscious or not.

Emotions, per se, do not have an independent existence absent the subject that experiences them. As noted, emotion qualia are generated and sustained by neuro-humoral mechanisms and exert unsuspected influence on our 'rational' analysis and conclusions during the decision-making process. The higher the emotional valence content of the stored memory the easier can it be retrieved into active conscious participation. Another neuro-anatomical region very poorly investigated is the neocortical, frontal lobe 'working memory' area 46 linking to the contiguous Broca Area during the elaboration of the 'silent speech' that accompanies thought. It is worth noting that arcuate fibers connect the working memory area 46 with the parieto-temporal angulat gyrus (Wernickes area 39) where audio-visual language input is being transmitted to Broca's area.

At what stage do emotional contents enter into an ongoing decision-making process? We may never be able to answer that question to satisfy our curiosity about its lack of significant negative influence in subjects that had previously lived under stress, illness and other circumstances that naturally breed contempt and ill feelings, we are referring to those few historical prophets living before the advent of the organized religions to guide and shape their own behaviors and that of others. Based on neuro-anatomical physiology data we are inclined to suspect that there may exist separate but dynamically interactive perceptual phenomenal and conceptual epistemological processes guided by the language faculty.

We have already visited the subconscious stage during the second-order context analysis where ongoing sensory inputs (body language, sounds, etc.) are played out in the context of emotional memories. We saw how, e.g., primary and secondary occipital audiovisual cortices exchange information with the temporal hippocampus formation via the inferior longitudinal fasciculus as this crosses the entorhinal cortex on its route to the central autonomic center and the hypothalamus, where involuntary reflex motor responses are coordinated. The problem may come when we register delayed information transfer (e.g., motor modifications?) into neo cortical representations that bypass the thalamic relay stations, as when the amygdala projects into frontal cortex and insula. The hippocampus also projects along fornix to hippo-thalamic mamillary bodies before it returns to anterior thalamus to control input synchronization into cingulate gyrus. The medial dorsal thalamic (MD) relay nucleus represents another important transitory gate to the prefrontal neocortex involved in the thalamo-cortical synchronization that possibly plays a role in the conscious playback rehearsal of probable pre-existing scenarios as coded for alternative responses in cortical attractor phase space. They play a role in dynamically modifying/updating and integrating these reservoirs of information as to their content of relevant emotional or cognitive content as it cascades into the decision-making process.

We speculate these pathways are more concerned with the decision-making process and, if associated with the beta wave of the EEG, it may well provide one of several still missing links connecting the brain with transfinity, whatever that may turn out to be?

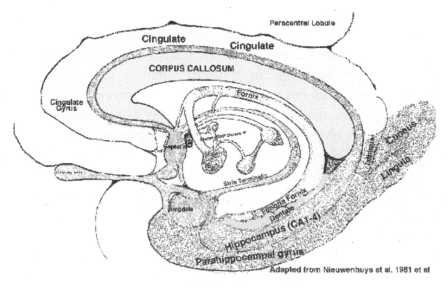

Limbic System

When we speak of the axiology of behavior we are exclusively referring to the universally accepted values in the self-conscious state, not the immanent affective pain/pleasure considerations that always guide subhuman species social behavior and often control the human individual actor. We do not inherit the qualia associated with our social behavior, we inherit the archetype first order representation whose phenotype quale expression is triggered and conditioned by the specific, ongoing neuro-humoral and biopsychosocial circumstances of the subject. Until someone is able to describe the 'God gene' we will assume that the secular-ethical and theological-moral values as such are, by and large, the result of learned behavioral standards and not the inherited non-conscious biological urge for food and sex satisfaction, the psychic feeling of well being and self-esteem, social acceptance and recognition. This distinction is critical because it suggests that, just like the practice and rehearsal of stereotyped reflex behavior and the concomitant recall of the associated positive emotional valence qualia forms good BPS habits and the same results can be argued for the formation of conditioned, ethically and morally-inspired reflex behaviors and neuro-chemically mediated good addictions! Again, since environmentally-acquired influences plays such an important role in such character formation, how did it happen to some special, selected few people living under so many adverse conditions at a time in history when such organized positive guidance and influences were absent. Was it a revelation reaching their brains? Originating where? Self generated or originating in transfinity? We have already taken the first steps to describe the probable reciprocal transactional information transfer pathways between the brain and transfinity.

During the elaboration of an attractor alternative subsequent to first and second order scrutiny of novel input stimuli arriving consciousness for further assessment as to its meaning to the subject's economy, the focusing is in the language parsing and selection of the conceptual content best explaining the meaning of the novelty at hand. The perceptual second order representations may be modified but only in later stages when the final selection of this alternative may be considered. Past the subconscious stage, we arrive at the stage of co-generation of thought and silent inner language content. We believe that the sequencing of all sensory inputs and their integration into one unit has already occurred and the focus now is on the cognitive epistemological aspects.

As previously noted, personal, family, neighborhood and cultural influences will provide the personality background against which a new unfamiliar situation will play out for comparison and judgment purposes before qualia considerations enter the picture. The subjects acquired cognitive ability to properly structure the language representations of the new situation, i.e., language of thought (LOT) symbolic or sentential representations of predicates of subject 'I', for comparison with an accepted ethical or moral standard, when available, will determine the righteousness of the decision outcome. And so will the neuro-muscular control of behavior expected to follow during its implementation. There may be pre-existing attractor solutions containing one or more such elements (e.g., conditioned responses, neuro-humoral and physical ability to implement response, emotional qualia, etc.) of the new situation awaiting a response. The most important considerations are usually not established on the basis of axiological righteousness of the selection but on plain biological survival and reproductive priorities such as the preprogrammed neuromuscular, neurohumoral considerations that effectively brings the expected movement to the intended target goal during execution. This means that the cortical premotor attractor probability being considered has to match the postural convenience and efficiency of movement as controlled by basal ganglia and cerebellum respectively. Adequate muscle tone and autonomic neuro-chemical control of involuntary muscles and glands are assumed even though decisions are made during the wakeful state when self consciousness is regained and postural gross and fine control of movements is accessible and ready to be willed into action by targets and goals that impose the appropriate muscle tone balance between agonists and antagonist effectors. Once a given response plan is willed the motor details of what follows in the execution is already compiled.

In other words, preceding the righteousness and correctness of behaviors in the decision-making process for selecting and initiating behavioral patterns out of the repertoire of cortical attractor probabilities, there are biological imperatives that control the selection, not to mention the psycho-social well being pressures likely to be generated during the selection. At the same time the language faculty is dynamically adjusting its inner language content to 'rationalize' and eventually report on the decision.

The generation of silent inner language at the beginning of the third order representation has two aspects. The motor aspect is based on the production of those sounds characterizing the chosen language framework being used (alphabet, syllables, phrases) during content generation. Somehow meanings result from the combination of sounds, language structure (positioning of subject, its predicates and syntax) and the corresponding conditioning behavior pre-programmed.

SUMMARY AND CONCLUSIONS

In general, it has been difficult for investigators to accept that, e.g., driving on a dangerous, but familiar, curvy road in the mountains while listening to a Brahms Symphony and talking to your wife on the cell phone requires only a self conscious effort in the cell phone. Of course a sudden unfamiliar rabbit crossing in front of the car or an unexpected dissonant note from the French horn may cause you to brake before going airborne beyond the cliff. This distinction between subconscious **awareness** and **self consciousness** is now accepted after distinguishing between so called *creature* consciousness and *mental-state* consciousness. The former is the garden variety wakeful state, intransitive variant (from sleep, coma or anesthesia) and the *mental-state* supposes the general intransitive state before targeting a particular transitional state.

Eventually investigators will need to address the issue of whether first order representations format is analog or has a fine-grained content. In our opinion what is more important is the indexical content of the ongoing unfamiliar situation (i.e., the 'what' and 'where' registered in primary sensory cortex and further refined by temporal cortex) and its immediate meaning to the subject. Causality and intentionality considerations preempt any other concern. This is followed by the response guiding system initiated at the parietal lobe and culminating at the pre-motor cortex.

The next distinction was between **subconscious** awareness of representations of, e.g., sensory phenomena or of beliefs/thoughts thereof, like when driving and talking on the cell phone? At a higher order level this distinction is related to the distinction between the third order sense-*phenomenal consciousness*, on the one hand—which is a property of states *that* it is *like something* to be in, that have a particular qualia distinctive 'feel' (See Nagel 1974)—and, on the other hand, metaphysical logic abstractions thereof based on universal ethical and moral values acquired by learning or revelation(?). A sort of special but undefined access consciousness being influenced by extrasensory sources of righteousness? (See Block 1995). Why rule out conscious access to non-phenomenal mental states of thoughts and judgments. We don't even know if phenomenal states as such, not our feelings and thought attributions, can be subject to reductive explanations in functional and/or other representational forms. What is important is the rational impact such language-based representations will have in the decision-making process, notwithstanding the continuous influence of negative valence emotional pressures.

One of the most fascinating developments in neuroscience comes from studies on prosthetic devices interfacing with brain tissue. Can a hand-held monitor (visual, auditive, tactile, etc.) send transduced signals to an electrode interfacing with the sensory cortex and transform, e.g., the visual sensation of an object or event being monitored, into the **same** phenomenal conscious attributions being monitored? The ongoing interpretation has it that eventually those monitored experiences acquire three-dimensional distal intentional contents in the brain, an alleged representation of the monitored positions and movements of same objects in space time, as if those patterns themselves become imbued with spatial content. The subjects report that it feels like the monitored object is moving., as if the subjects' first-order intentional perceptual contents have not quite become that different and that they all acquire a dimension of seeming or subjectivity. Quite a feat for the subject's theory of mind! We posit that, if the camera electrodes are placed on a different primary sensory area the results reported will reflect more on that location (place theory) and will not be so dependent on the afferent information input from the camera monitor. But those experiments have not being performed yet.

Dr. Angell O. de la Sierra, Esq. In Deltona, Florida Spring, 2012.

REFERENCES

1. Baars, B., 1988. *A Cognitive Theory of Consciousness*. Cambridge: Cambridge University Press

2. Block, N. and Stalnaker, R., 1999. 'Conceptual analysis, dualism and the explanatory gap,' *Philosophical Review*, 108: 1-46.

3. Carruthers, P. and Veillet, B., 2007. 'The phenomenal concept strategy,' *Journal of Consciousness Studies*, 14 (9-10).

4. Chalmers, D., 1996. *The Conscious Mind*. Oxford: Oxford University Press

5. Dennett, D., 1991. *Consciousness Explained*. London: Allen Lane.

6. Fodor, J., 1990. *A Theory of Content and Other Essays*. Cambridge, MA: MIT Press.

7. Lau, H. and Rosenthal, D., 2011. 'Empirical support for higher-order theories of conscious awareness,' *Trends in Cognitive Sciences*, 15: 365-373.

8. Picciuto, V., 2011. 'Addressing higher-order misrepresentation with quotational thought,' *Journal of Consciousness Studies*, 18(3-4): 109-136.

9. Weisberg, J., 2011. 'Abusing the notion of what-it's-like-ness: A response to Block,' *Analysis*, 71: 438-443.

 Source of Righteousness

The Subconscious Perceptual and Conceptual Content and its Conscious (Epistemological) Linguistic Representation

The Living Prophet

INTRODUCTION

An intelligent engineering design of a thermostat only requires it to become electronically **aware** of changes in local environmental temperature in relation to a standard, preprogrammed reference scale and report the fluctuations with visible warnings (digitally or otherwise) to an observer. More complex industrial ones may, in addition to the standard 'inherited' scale, include access to a 'memory' database coding for comparisons with previously recorded variations for that season in that geographical location, the basis for the activation of sophisticated preprogrammed audio-visual alerting signals when a match is found. Should there be unexpected temperatures outside the range designed for the unit, the thermostat 'brain' will either freeze or burn with no recourse to articulate adjustments not previously programmed and choose from among probable alternatives the best adaptive solution to preserve its structural/functional integrity. This scenario would be the equivalent of an adaptive decision-making process, triggered by either external or body-proper sensory organs (like the smart thermostat) rooted exclusively on unconscious genetic and subconscious memetic pre-programmed input resources for subhuman species to efficiently deal with the real time quotidian existential reality contingencies in their ecosystem that may threaten their biological integrity. Subhuman species evolve by completing a life cycle until eventual entropy-guided, genetically programmed extinction ensues, so recorded history tells us.

The human species would share a similar evolutionary cyclic path were it not for its exclusive ability to introspectively discover self as distinct from its surroundings, a significant advantage over completing our life cycle by reflexly executing whatever adaptive responses inherited genes and environmentally acquired memes have programmed us for. This introspective ability makes it possible to search for the **meaning** of the novel survival threats and the danger it represents to the species 'in general' and to the 'individualized' existential reality circumstance in particular. The results will make possible a response with novel adaptive survival solutions not previously scripted/anticipated in the genetic/memetic data bases. We have discussed in detail elsewhere the mechanisms triggering both the inherited unconscious reflex responses to familiar environmental objects/events involving amygdaloidal complex and the acquired subconscious responses involving hippocampus memory 'context' analysis. We have also discussed how, when the potentially threatening object/event was novel, we had to access the Wernicke-Broca complex language faculty to co-generate silent language and thought and thereby code and improvise the novel adaptive solutions that resulted in strategies to be consciously willed into execution, those with the highest probability of adaptive success. See Vol. I, II "Neurophilosophy of Consciousness" at http://delaSierra-Sheffer.net.

We now speculate further on the details of the possible brain mechanisms involved in the cooperation between the phenomenal ontological and the conceptual epistemological (first and second order) neural network representations in the generation of the consciously willed hybrid decision-making alternative. We also need to expand further on the neuro-humoral underpinnings of the emotional influence on co-participating logic processes and some of the controversial premises and predictions involved.

ARGUMENTATION

We need not, at this juncture, to consider the important difference between the crucial transit from the 'subconscious state of awareness' we share with subhuman species to the exclusively human introspective state of 'self consciousness'. In fact we believe there may not even be a general state but an 'as needed' individualized mental state of either 'self consciousness' or subconscious awareness in humans. Unless novel BPS threatening object/events enter our phenomenal threshold of sensory awareness detection we continue to operate on subconscious mode, like when traveling along a familiar but dangerous mountain roads when driving to work or the market while concentrating on radio news from, e.g., the 'awakening' Middle East militia turbulence. We thus assume the premise of a previous attainment of the 'general' self conscious mental state prior to the focusing on the individualized existential circumstance of being challenged by the potential danger of a sudden, novel, ongoing, real time, ontological, sense-phenomenal object/event or the sudden epistemological, memory-derived but transitory presence of its (first or second order) mental abstract representation. To narrow the scope of this brief analysis we need be concerned only on the search for an adaptive, logically-based, conceptually universal, abstract model to interact and influence this second order abstract representation (of the preceding first order phenomenal representation of existential, sensory or memory based experience of real-time reality).

Pure phenomenal awareness of **familiar** sensory objects or events is transitory (working memory) and need not reach but fleeting consciousness of their physical brain network presence or their causal influence in any response; same for transitory, memory-based flashes. However, when **unfamiliar**, as determined by the subconscious amygdale/hippocampus preceding 'context' scrutiny, the next step requires enabling the access to the language faculty to extract its conscious meaning to the body economy. The language faculty will mobilize the organism's decision-making processes (see Dretske, Block 1995) which includes the rationalization of the event to the extent possible based on the subject's previous personal ethical/moral experiences or beliefs, acquired or 'revealed'? At this stage, the subject's subconscious awareness is reductively analyzed and represented with the appropriate logic symbols/sentence with the help of the language faculty. This will cogenerate thought and an inner, silent proto language explanation of **meaning** in terms of a causal role, intentional content and biopsychosocial well being parameters before being stored as a probable solution to be consciously free willed from among other alternatives present in the pre motor cortical attractor phase space.

To illustrate, the sequence starts with a phenomenal unconscious awareness of e.g., a novel red object when chatting while driving in the mountain road. The blind sight equivalent of the red object is first subjected to a safety scrutiny by the amygdaloid complex, followed by a subconscious road environment 'context' analysis (memory) by the hippocampus system. We have witnessed the transition from the unconscious genetic domain to the subconscious genetic plus memetic domain. Absent previous information about such new red object it is then subjected to a conscious analysis to establish its **meaning** to the subject's body biopsychosocial economy. We are now witnessing the transition from the subconscious awareness domain to the self-conscious domain. This new mental stage consists, among other things, in thoughts about, e.g., redness of previous actions that are guided by redness. This phenomenal consciousness of the new object and its meaning to the subject may vary in its degree of elaboration into silent but reportable language depending on its circumstantial context to the extent that its explanation may become ineffable, or indescribable because it does not match any fitting, indexically precise conceptual or perceptual analog, e.g., the sudden appearance of a strange red object in the skies as opposed to watching it holding my hand. The red color in abstract is different from that indexically precise 'That red object I am viewing now'. When indexically imprecise redness may be associated with ethical or moral standards/codes, e.g., red traffic lights, red blood, red underwear, etc., the richness of the content—acquired or revealed(?) experience—will have an impact on the 'righteousness' content in the decision-making process. This underscores the importance of moral theological or ethics secular education during the early formative years.

In the cortical attractor phase space we find the convergence of mental-state types consisting of both conscious perceptual and conceptual varieties. We find it hard to believe that phenomenal attributes in **abstract**, like beliefs and desires can be **exclusively** activated unconsciously. Attributes, phenomenal or qualia, of physical objects or subjects do not have an independent existence. What we are trying to question is, whether we can linguistically conceptualize directly from a previous first order, e.g., visual phenomenal object, or even a second order abstraction when situated in a background context? The language-based conceptualization is an attempt to extract BPS meaning for the subject. Repeating, the brain can only have **first order** representations of physical, sensory detected or imagined objects/events which are unconsciously subjected to an amygdaloid, genetically-based analysis as explained. The moment we follow-up with a subsequent 'context' analysis by the hippocampus, memory-based complex we will have completed a **second order** representation at the subconscious stage. Only when dealing with unfamiliar, novel objects/events do we access the language faculty to provide a transitory meaning to the body economy in a **third order** representation.

If we ignore for the moment the first order creative activity inspired by imagined **phenomenal** colored objects by creative artists like, e.g., Tina York, let's consider the different case when the first order representation was exclusively a **non-phenomenal** abstract figment of her imagination, like the poems that frequently follow her paintings? Usually, these conceptual representations are based on **second or higher order** distortions (willed or pathological) of memory data. Here is what we can learn from experimental clinical observations.

Can a person 'see' an 'invisible' micro object shown (or 'revealed'?) to him? Or, what type of a mental representation, if any, can a subject make of an existing physical object yet invisible to him, e.g., when he had a portion of his **primary** visual cortex damaged and cannot see/describe the essential or attributive elements of any physical object placed in the visual field of the damaged region? The latter is the condition of 'blind sight' discovered by Carruthers in 1996. However, these same subjects can accurately and consistently distinguish horizontal from vertical lines placed in the same visual field! Yet, they cannot verbally report this occurrence. This to us is the difference between their subconscious 'awareness' potential and a normal subject's reportable 'consciousness' of self and the same object which he is able to conceptualize and verbally report even in the object's absence. We dare not guess on the details of what kind of first or second order conceptualization was possible, if any. Likewise, there are other patients with **visual agnosia** (no conscious visual experience) yet their perceptual capacities to describe attributive colors and textures (of what?) are preserved. It suggests that the perceptual temporal lobe locus is spared and distinguished from the damaged conceptual parietal lobe locus. This data makes us believe in the existence of cooperating but **independent** second order representations of the perceptual and the conceptual and the importance of consciousness to activate the language faculty in elaborating a **third order** conceptual representation of the preceding novel **second order** sense-phenomenal input whereas the familiar perceptual representation (first or second order), however transitory, is present at subconscious levels. We dare not guess the detailed features of the temporal lobe perceptual representation or the presumed absence of the conceptual representation at the parietal lobe locus associated with consciousness and the language faculty. The only clue we have is that the brain's parietal angular gyrus locus receives information inputs from primary sensory areas before relaying the information to Wernicke and Brocas areas, both associated with proto language elaboration. The parietal lobes influence the control of ongoing, real time sense phenomenal perceptual responses to ontological/existential contingencies; whereas the temporal lobes are primarily concerned with epistemological considerations of the meanings of preceding or simultaneous object/event perceptual recognition/learning. Only the perceptual representations generated by the temporal-lobe system we are phenomenally conscious of and reportable. On the other hand the temporal-lobe is supposed to have access both to property information and to spatial information. This is an important distinction between an ontological 'what-where-when' locus in the temporal lobes and a decision-making 'how-to', 'action-guiding' locus originating in the parietal lobes. Yet, all things considered, why is it that having arrived at the most logical conclusion about an adequate response to a novel situation, most people will compromise and, depending on real time, existential and ongoing biopsychosocial circumstances, a neurohumoral-instantiated emotion will control the decision making process? See Vol. III, "Neurophilosophy of Consciousness." for a more detailed analysis. We will now summarize the salient points that may suggest a lateralization of hemispheric controls of decision-making processes which may explain why a background of formally acquired ethical/moral early experiences resist better the emotional hijacking in the last stages of the decisional process. This is also characteristic of the epistemological, universals-centered control of decision-making showed and recorded for the historical prophets long before the existence of the Abrahmic theologies. How did they acquire that guidance and orientation, by revelation?

With the advent of FMRI technology and the data from brain lesion studies we have been able to document that while Emotions are complex and involve a variety of adaptive physical and cognitive responses to environmental stimulus, the study has provided good evidence for the asymmetric nature of brain hemispheric functions in humans. We can at least generalize and say that most language production and processing occur in the left hemisphere and most of the emotional production and processing occurs in the right hemisphere. There is some confusion in the literature because of the non-specific, liberal use of terms. Subjective qualia depends on the conscious third order conceptualization of emotions requiring the introspective identification of self as the subject of that feeling. As explained above, a novel object, event or delusional thought are groups belonging to the same class of **unfamiliar** entities and share an initial first order brain representation and a subsequent second order representation when processed for its contextual background. Conscious processing to extract their meaning and their subsequent language representation in terms of logical symbols and sentential equivalents represents the third order stage. The processing and production of physical facial expressions of emotions may be subconscious and also appear to be asymmetric in nature, the left side (right hemisphere-dominant) showing better effector responses. Here is some of what medical research has found to substantiate the possible independent existence of perceptual and conceptual interacting brain data bases.

A person lacking his right, <u>prefrontal lobe</u> because of a surgical excision or otherwise also lacked decision-making skills especially when confronted with immediate BPS well being vs. future consequences of reward or punishment. He would always settle for immediate results (usually reward), like subjects lacking early ethical/moral experiences at an early age. Researchers in these cases were also able to successfully use <u>conditioning</u> based on **verbal** stimuli containing emotional meaning where **non-verbal** strategies failed.

<u>Schizophrenic</u>s show an increase in right hemispheric lateralization and an increase in left handedness. The loss of left hemispheric control is evidenced by their difficulty in processing many of aspects of language and speech, including prosody.

Besides its known role in the unconscious genetic-based processing of stimulus threatening the biological integrity of the human species by the right <u>amygdala,</u> the left counterpart also participates in the self conscious presence of emotional qualia. There may be a neurohumoral control of emotional <u>Valence</u> asymmetry where <u>cholinergic</u> and <u>dopaminergic</u> neurohormones exercise control of the left hemisphere and <u>noradrenergic</u>s control the right hemisphere counterpart.

It is also noteworthy that the reliable skin conductance response (<u>SCR</u>) to emotional qualia is significantly diminished by right hemispheric damage to brain's anterior <u>supramarginal gyrus</u> and posterior <u>angular gyrus</u> regions while damage to the opposite left hemispheric parietal counterpart did not. Likewise, fMRI clearly showed an activation of the temporal lobe right <u>superior temporal gyrus</u> during the processing of happiness-producing stimulation while the left <u>pulvinar</u> showing increases only when responding to fearful stimuli. It is not clear why the right pulvinar is activated during aversive conditioning. It is fair to say that emotions are processed in many parts of the brain and that emotions are very complex entities to analyze.

SUMMARY AND CONCLUSIONS

We hope to have partially answered the 'what' is it about a **conscious** phenomenal perception that makes it worth the attention that triggers the conceptual data base into activity, something that a blindsight perceptual state would correspondingly lack. A phenomenally aware subconscious state is different from a self-conscious phenomenal state in that the former are second order representations of perceptual data and the latter are third order representations when novel and in need of further elaboration to find their existential meaning with the assistance of the language faculty.

We reserve the unconscious states, or **first order** representations thereof, to genetically inherited patterns of adaptive responses to situations (sensory or imagined objects/events) potentially challenging the integrity of the biological structure and function of the species, regardless of their fineness of grain and richness of content. When it becomes necessary to identify the contextual background behind the object an additional memory resource, (memetic) is added as the culmination of the subconscious state, or **second order** representations thereof.

If the situation is unfamiliar or novel, a meaning to the BPS economy is searched for by accessing the language faculty and thereby attaining the conscious state, or **third order** representation thereof. Depending on the perceptual or conceptual content and its fineness of grain, the perceptual can be further conceptualized and/or the conceptual can be further refined using in both cases symbolic or sentential **fourth order** representations when preparing explanatory models. Relevant meanings derived from the cooperation of perceptual and conceptual databases converge and gradually evolve into an option as a belief-like alternative of either a theological or scientific adaptive response.

This explanation may explain how the subconscious perceptual awareness guides movement in the agnosia patient and is substantially different from the conceptual counterpart during the generation of belief and thought as aided by the silent language elaboration. (see also Lau and Rosenthal 2011). There are circumstances in which people's subjective, self conscious reports of visual experiences, are impaired while their unconscious first-order and/or subconscious discrimination abilities remain fully intact. Interestingly, their visual consciousness in these conditions is specifically associated with activity in a region of the dorsolateral prefrontal cortex where we have posited as the anatomical location of the attractor phase space. (See Rounis et al. 2010) describing how the transcranial magnetic stimulation directed at that cortical area disrupts its functioning without impairing unconscious first-order or subconscious second order task performance.

A final decision is a phenomenally conscious mental state, when freely consented to, among alternatives in cortical attractor spaces, i.e., a meaningful **fourth order** mental state that resulted from the preceding conscious **third order** language representation scrutiny in search for an alternate or new adaptive response to a relevant and significant **new** contingency. In the **absence** of novelty, needless to say, a purely conceptual belief or a virtual image representation of a perceptual, fleeting past object or event in working memory gives rise to **second order** subconscious representations without there ever being any concurrent phenomenally perceptual event physically present. We feel it is necessary that **third order** states include perceptual states, mental images, bodily sensations, and emotional feelings that are all phenomenally conscious because they are now emerging adaptive alternatives blending and comparing the subconscious content with their corresponding analog or conceptual equivalent in memory. It does not matter much whether the final consented to higher-order perception is experienced as an 'inner-sense' quale or a higher-order thought or belief, they both, ultimately are accompanied by a feeling of BPS well being unless we are describing the historical prophets and their recorded acts contra self interest and well being. Both perceptual and conceptual states of second order subconscious awareness functionally become the third order self conscious state by virtue of their dynamic interaction, i.e., the higher-order thought/mental state evolves by virtue of the conceptual state being the actual target of the perceptual state to form an adaptive viable hybrid alternative for free will to choose from. It is important to remember that cortical attractor probable solutions, higher order representations are dynamic and interactive until one is finally chosen for execution.

In our human existential reality we may experience vague **first-order** non-conceptual qualia unrelated to any meaningful causal relation to perceptions from our environments and bodies. But we may also have **second-order** non-conceptual qualia based on incorporation of additional content, learned experience related to the first-order state. This may take the form of a non conscious scanning of the environment/body (inner sense) to produce fine-grained representations that can then serve to ground thoughts for subsequent integration with the conceptual data base in the conscious **third order** elaboration of an adaptive action-plan, a higher-order representation of those integrated inputs. See John Locke 1690.

The question remains, can it be falsifiably established how the influence of early childhood theological indoctrination on ethical and moral value systems establishes an eventual reservoir for consciously accessible, metaphysical logic, coded source of left-hemispheric universal values to mediate and positively influence the real time, ongoing decision-making process of existential reality? For those historical prophets who lacked the experience of ethical and moral indoctrination, what was their source of righteousness? Revelations? If so, we have already outlined the neural pathways to reciprocally transfer information from the transfinity source to the relevant left hemispheric locus. See Vol. III, "Neurophilosophy of Consciousness." at http://delaSierra-Sheffer.net and http://angelldls.wordpress.com/.

Dr. Angell O. de la Sierra, Esq. In Deltona, Florida Winter 2011.

5 The Epistemontology of Friendship and Love

Ataraxia vs. Apatheia

Armor Dark Saber

INTRODUCTION

The recent hurtful experience of witnessing the painful journey of my son from a moribund state into the irreversible death and transfiguration and the concomitant expressions of empathy and love from friends and family everywhere gave me the opportunity to reflect further on the co-existence of both abstract metaphysical and practical existential aspects of transcultural love and friendship as recently identified in the various expressions of condolences from family and friends worldwide, all now briefly analyzed below from a biopsychosocial perspective. Because of the wide transcultural spectrum, ranging from my readers I have never personally met to biological filiations, I am trying myself to understand if friendship and love qualia may be an essential part of the inherited and/or acquired survival instinct or does it transcend the primitive function of keeping the human species together for the common defense against survival threats against their collective biopsychosocial integrity in order to guarantee the survival and continuation of the species to reproductive age and beyond. Or is it part and parcel of another metaphysical, impersonal, apatheic logical elaboration of the language faculty that expresses a ratification of value and commitment to defend universal values and entities as varied as other species, objects, principles or goals? This metaphysical language processing conceptualize into analytical, abstract, symbolic and sentential representations (metaphors) of the real time existential experience of the grieving actor (whether inherited, acquired and 'revealed') which will stoically and dispassionately bear on his decision making processes to rationalize the painful quale when accessed? Does it express an abstract but genuine love or an equally genuine existential friendship? Is there a difference? Do we need to choose or do we consciously will, as an adaptive defense mechanism, an ataraxic state to mediate but inevitably execute a compromise between the ontologically, existentially experienced angst and the epistemologically, rationally idealized in abstraction? Before we proceed further in this brief analysis, we need to know what is the western cultural norm for describing existential love.

Quoting from 1 Cor. 13:4-7, NIV, Apostle Paul described love in the famous poem in 1 Corinthians, thus: "Love is patient, love is kind. It does not envy, it does not boast, it is not proud. It is not rude, it is not self-seeking, it is not easily angered, it keeps no record of wrongs. Love does not delight in evil but rejoices with the truth. It always protects, always trusts, always hopes, and always perseveres." It is self-evident this metaphysical universals-laden quote does **not** describe the behavior of most of us mortal members of the human species. This kind of conscious **impersonal** behavior is drawing heavily from **both** co-existing, neutrally valence-coded brain data bases. What guides a human being to preferentially transcend his pitiful real time human existence and learn also to **objectively** love those objects, principles, or goals they value greatly and are deeply commit themselves to their defense and preservation even when it is possibly threatening their own preservation, e.g., the historical prophets? This is to be distinguished from the essentially **subjective, emotional, consciously interpersonal** bonding outreach of some volunteers with e.g., objects, political or spiritual convictions, animals, etc. This should not be confused with psychopathological cases of paraphilia where sexual delusions become part of the subjects mindset.

ARGUMENTATION AND CONCLUSIONS

We have all experienced the **interpersonal** expressions of love at the ontological level as essentially a biological human effort, not very different from the extinction of hunger or thirst driven by neuro-hormones and characterized by probable sexual attraction and attachment. The latter is better characterized as the psycho-social and cultural acquired component influenced also in its instantiation or embodiment by hormones promoting an experience of mental well being, e.g., oxytocin, vasopressin, neurotrophins, pheromones, etc. The signs and symptoms of this physiological arousal are characterized by transitory, trivial cardio-respiratory dysfunction. An important variation of this interpersonal element is that seen when the epistemological component is in control, i.e., where the experience of affectionate feeling of intimacy and empathy is **not** accompanied by physiological arousal. Is the emotional component totally absent? Quare. When my international friends from HiQ listings and extended distant family that I have not seen or heard from for a long time send cards and e-mails of condolences, do they truthfully say what they mean and mean what they say or is it just a culturally-imposed, emotionally-neutral protocol/language script being followed?

Interestingly, in my mental perambulations in search of tranquility and adequacy of response to suffering, I discovered the Pyrrhonians epistemological approach most convenient because the situation could be handled in theory as an **impersonal** relation because, why assume the love expressions from the stranger are not truly qualia experienced by the sender? Why not suspend judgment on dogmatic cultural or theological beliefs in the absence of factual evidence or credible intuitions? But more important, one can rationalize the situation and ask the Epicureans question, why should I worry about an intention I do not even know it exists? This was the same type of rational liberation from the anguish of the unknown I managed to experience when viewing the dying scenario of my son before my teary eyes, a sort of conscious self-induced tranquil apatheia as long as I have no **rational** way to establish either the physical torment of my dead son or the truth of the intentions of the condolence senders. In retrospect, if I have consistently acted with respect, consideration, praised the trustworthy, being compassionate and affectionate with dissenting colleagues and friends and consciously have practiced virtuosity (most of the times J), why should I worry? If I have consciously behaved that way I need not be concerned about the valence of love and friendship of others as long as I am able to love and be a good, friendly sentient being. This conscious, tranquil mental state is described by the Greeks as the 'ataraxic' state.

Is this the functional role of the metaphysical, logic-based, universally valued metaphor abstractions that the language faculty codes for our human species to consciously(?) access when in need to search for an adaptive BPS tranquil state, however immanent and transient?

In closing, a note to my local and international friends, family and colleagues, please accept my sincere thanks for your cards, phone calls and e-mails offering your condolences for the untimely death of our beloved son. Your thoughtfulness will be long remembered.

CHAPTER 6

The Epistemontology of Life and Existence

Death and Transfiguration

INTRODUCTION

We, as individuals, seem to be controlled by two, often disparate, existential systems, each endowed with its own distinct strategy when processing the idea of life and the circumstance of quotidian, real time existence and death. Both existential mind sets, conscious and subconscious, respectively, can significantly change our behavioral approach toward unexpected contingencies such as actually coming face to face with impending death and suffering. The epistemological/ abstract eternal and the ontological/individualized

44

experiential, clash in both attitudes and actions as the will works out adaptive solutions in very different—almost opposite—ways. The coexistence of both conscious and subconscious strategies comes dramatically into life when experiencing and/or witnessing the metaphysical and emotional evolution of a human death.

ARGUMENTATION

Life. Many years back when I was a young Catholic biophysicist at Sloan-Kettering Institute for Cancer Research I was very curious about how a crystalline ribonucleic acid powder (Rous Sarcoma Virus or RSV) standing in a test tube for weeks could come alive when cultured with chick embryo fibroblasts. I wanted to capture and describe that crucial moment of animation by using serial measurements with the latest biophysical chemistry technology including electron microscopy. I was lost and threw the towel when RSV disappeared from cytoplasm and incorporated itself into host nuclear DNA. Soon afterwards Howard and Temin won a Nobel prize by describing how RNA transcriptase enabled the viral replication based on similar results. At that time I simply called the RSV crystal a 'truncated life' who hijacked the host cell's reproductive machinery for its own cancerous replicating ends. I then decided to come back to that enigma, in a neurophilosophical broad context, upon retirement from academia. After three published volumes on a model of brain dynamics the problem has become more complex than I had bargained for as will be briefly discussed below. The main Gordian knot has been an un-necessary quest by physical scientists and metaphysical theologians alike for a monadic interpretation of life at the exclusion of the other. Our contribution has been to argue for both sides of the same coin.

Scientific methodology has failed to explain how life, albeit in apparent or presumed abeyance of the first and second law of thermodynamics, is able to spontaneously evolve into a complex structural and dynamic entity able to self-generate and sustain a super-complex intrinsic order; all allegedly without the benefit of a preceding blueprint for such specific destiny. The fundamental transition from inorganic/organic atoms and molecules into a living unit of life still remains a fundamental mystery in physics, chemistry, and biology because of a lack of empirically complete and consistent descriptions or explanations of life as an emergent, irreducible and animated fact of nature. One can understand why the comfort of giving some rest to an unsatisfied inquiring mind by resting the case on a convenient "self-replicating" DNA which understandably has evolved into a major metaphor for explaining **all** there is to be learned about life. After all, why not invoke coding self-replicators and coded self-organizing interactors at all levels of organization to counteract the inescapable and self-evident causally efficient but invisible driving force which seems to be controlling evolution by natural selection? However, it is just as counter-intuitive to analytical logic to conceptualize humans as survivalist epiphenomenal gene-vehicles, a la Dawkins, as it is to invoke the exclusive mediation of an intelligent design or blueprint guiding such beautiful and complex order defying natural laws as witnessed in developmental and evolutionary biology. What is life then? Let's first agree on the terminology, what do we mean by 'life', 'existence', 'essential' as opposed to 'accidental' attributions and others.

Having personally witnessed the early death and transfiguration of my dear son John Arthur, I had the opportunity to differentiate between that conceptualized instant of animation of matter when 'life' comes into being, like the RSV ribonucleoprotein described above, and that subsequent, perceptual description of 'life in transit' I chose to call 'existence' in real time.

Central to 'life' is its scientific characterization of 'existence' as essentially open-ended systems **yet** subtly maintained in steady states **yet** far from an equilibrium and sustained by a self-regulated inflow/outflow of matter/energy to fuel self-regulated auto-catalytic smaller cycles. The latter are somehow programmed to complete a much larger human life cycle of simultaneously conjoined endergonic negentropy and exergonic entropy. In the beginning of the cycle—endergonic control phase—we sense and respond to internal and external environments, we extract energy, build and generate complex sub-systems at a faster rate than at a later exergonic control phase where we degrade energy, deconstruct and degenerate at faster rates as we complete our human cycle of life, happiness, suffering and eventual death. Living is dying.

As we learn more and more about the biophysical chemistry of living organisms we seem to be in denial that, because we cannot ontologically describe either a causally efficient force to drive the dynamics of the living or the essential negentropy of structural/functional details of its self-evident order, there must exist an epistemological metaphysical entity providing the blueprints for their orderly evolution into a living unit. So, why not ignore those two postulates of scientific methodology and invoke the mysterious existence of autopoietic, self generating, self sustaining super-complex activity that, equally mysteriously 'emerges' into a super-complex living unit. As such that miracle of creation is seen as being somehow essentially endowed with another super-complex genetic and memetic memory database good for a human life cycle. A materialistic act of faith and denial! So much for the super-complexity of the enactment of life from the non-living.

What about the evolutionary path of the living unit as it unfolds in real space-time? Do we evolve according to the exclusively rational ontological model of the materialistic faith or the exclusively epistemological model of the theological faith? What kind of decision-making behavior, should we predict from either model? Are there other alternatives? Stay tuned. See also Harold 2001.

It has not been so bad for an ontological scientific model of 'life' rooted essentially on falsifiable sense-phenomenal measurements on the one hand and intuitions about experiences on invisible and significant objects and/or events whose existential meaning is epistemologically found when expressed and communicated in a metaphysical logic language, on the other hand. A hybrid model of sorts. But which side of the epistemontological coin do we choose? Do we need to have choices?

Existence. Contrary to the experience of the originally elongated chick embryo fibroblast that predictably transformed into a spherical tumor cell within the standard environmental condition (STP) of the experiment, in the exclusive case of the human species, existence is an individualized self conscious experience of being oneself—as distinct from the relevant sense-phenomenal or intuited invisible surroundings which become the human existential circumstance. The human existence is predicated on inherited, acquired or willfully (or not) created circumstances. The latter does not exclude circumstances from being consciously willed (or not) as imaginary, mythical, fictional, and the like. To say that it 'exists' means/ implies it is 'real' for a self-conscious person within a stated probability. If the object/event is a pathognomonic reality of mental disease it is **not** proper to say it 'exists'. If something 'is', whether ontologically sensed or epistemologically inferred as probable (not possible!) under specified STP conditions, then it 'exists' under the scrutiny of metaphysical logic methods even if invisible to the sensory detection. In other words, existence implies a probable predicate attribution of an entity that 'is', ontologically measured matter or epistemologically inferred micro because of extrasensory dimensions. It is important to distinguish further between the existential—as defined—and the predicative context. There is an essential and an accidental predicate. A particulate matter is an **essential** predicate—invisible or not—whereas a wave form is an **accidental** predicate expressing the manner in which the particulate matter travels in space time. Color, shape, etc. are examples of accidental, non-essential predicates. Of more common use are, unfortunately, **identity** predicates where equivalent essential or accidental features are substituted for the original and then the **representation** handled as if they existed in reality and not analogically, a serious categorical error often found in the literature. Thus man is **essentially** a genetically determined biological entity with environmentally determined, acquired **accidental** predicates such as temperament, color, stature, and other psychosocial attributions. It should be obvious that once there exist accidental predicates there has to be an implied essential predicate because the former cannot have an independent existence. Man is he and his circumstance, a truly biopsychosocial (BPS) hybrid with free will. Without an introspective self consciousness-based free will one can conceive of a BPS adapted sub-human living being whose behavior or decision making process can be explained by Skinnerian operant conditioning or simulated in a computer. It is both the introspective capacity and the consequent co-generation of a silent language and thought that is exclusively human, as argued elsewhere. Having outlined the primacy of the genetically driven **biological** imperative of self preservation under unconscious control as an **essential** predicate and the memetically driven **accidental** predicate of his **psycho-social** existential circumstances under subconscious control, we should be in a position to generalize a model predicting the decision-making process for the human species. Which aspect will carry more weight in the free willing of behavioral adaptive alternatives, the rational or the emotional? Not so. The human species has been able to transcend the coded alternatives programmed in his genetic and memetic data bases and improvise a very individualized adaptive response tailored to his ongoing existential circumstance at that particular instance, sometime contrary to his own BPS interests. When you objectively ponder on this scenario you will realize that the materialistic, physicalist approach rooted exclusively on scientific methodology, while necessary and persuasive, is not sufficient to adequately model the dynamics of life and existence. We need to complement the physical evolutionary approach with a metaphysical component that will reach outside our 4-d space time for answers as explored in one of our dissertations. Of course, one can always settle for a myopic invocation of the magic of multiple autopoetic, self generated and self sustained forces that magically and spontaneously 'emerge' into a super complexity that violates the very physico-mathematical foundations of the physicalist rational approach. What role do non-rational, emotional circumstances play in the survival of our human species?

Death and Transfiguration. As my teary eyes watched my son Johnny die I kept asking to myself when does life end? Does life refer more to the functional integrity of the metabolic machinery sustaining the vital homeostatic processes like cell respiration and generation or does it mean the sudden or gradual extinction of that integrated 'animation' of matter we normally describe as being 'alive'. For most of us parents, it is more like experiencing an irreversible harrowing process where both aspects, the biological chronicle of 'systems failure' and the sudden extinction of all measurable indices of animation. The former **described** by the physical credo that models the scientific physicalist script, the latter **explained** by the metaphysical script that models the theological credo. This inextricable duality makes life and death impossible to disambiguate. Having accepted death as a permanent, irreversible event, it now looks like the virtual mirror image of birth and life is seen now as 'something' that moves in and out of matter. But we may synthesize complex matter in the laboratory but never living/animated matter as described above. The combination of gametes DNA at fertilization to 'synthesize' living matter always has required a living cellular environment. Perhaps we will never know. As I pondered and grieved I turned my focus on the comparative effects of this ongoing process on the dying and myself on two levels. The first level was an evaluation of the efficacy of interspecies information transfer between Johnny and me. The second level was a speculation as to his suffering vis a vis my own. It did not take long for me to realize that the un-natural analgesic and anxiolytic pharmacological effects on both observed and observer respectively would seriously interfere with our cortical pre-motor mirror neurons and limbic systems as amply discussed elsewhere. When he was still in denial of the seriousness of his condition, his facial musculature profile and mental alertness reflected his hopes for recovery. When he was close to death his facial musculature relaxed as his mindscape revealed confusion and/or acceptance of his condition; at one point he even smiled. Not being able to analyze much at the first level, I turned into a speculation as to whether towards the end he was still suffering at least as much as I did. I was surprised at what a self-induced rationalization of the ongoing experience can do. At that point it became much more clear the distinction between the unconscious, subconscious and introspective self-consciousness aided by the co-generation of silent language and thought. I re-discovered, as hinted in a previous publication, that ultimately, rationalization of existential reality is a self serving activity geared to provide an experience of biopsychosocial well being, an epicurean hedonistic goal!! To follow are the tentative arguments I fashioned inside the Hospice room on that Sunday before he finally died.

Nobody wants their lives to end unless it is premature, the case of Johnny. But 'it' can move in at birth and out of existence at death, i.e. if there is re-incarnation, life is like an intervening gap of non-instantiated hibernation, a sort of break from 'existence' in the real, dangerous world and will continue in a paradisiac sleep waiting for a subsequent second or third, coming . . . Epicurus is smiling in his animated hibernation!

Epicurus characterized death as a harrowing evil but then rationalized: to whom? Not to Johnny, death will not affect him because when alive it is absent and when it comes he is absent. For death to harm the subject who dies, there must exist a *subject* who is harmed by death to satisfy its causal efficiency. Furthermore, who can precise the nature of the *harm* and the *time and place* where that harm is materialized? Restating, when the subject is alive there is no death and after we die there is no living subject to be harmed. Ergo, grief is entirely self-centered, me, the father, who wrapped inside a blanket of self-pity guilt emotionally grieve at my possible indirect, un-intentional involvement in his demise. But Johnny's body and mind are not harmed by its own extinction. If we ponder hard and find out we did everything a parent can do to preserve his life we can be harmed only by whatever real negative deeds that will cause us to suffer. Is this the unavoidable, self serving or self preserving BPS integrity function of self consciousness, to rationalize an escape hatch and survive as a species. We have examined in detail how humans can logically analyze a situation in abstract, with the best of our analytical faculties during a decision-making contingency, only to find out how the individualized, ongoing, real time existential reality hijacks the logical justifications in providing the subject with a feeling of biopsychosocial equilibrium and a sense of well being. Needless to say, this behavior maybe illegal, immoral and in the long run may constitute an act against self interest but this is not always the case where altruistic acts against self preservation interests are in conscious control of the decision-making brain circuitry. There have been recently published (last week!) fMRI studies on decision-making choice of alternatives demonstrating the individualized nature of these processes where ongoing, real time experiences seem to counter well thought analytical conclusions in the subjects tested. If the experience and peremptory satisfaction of a sense of biopsychosocial well being controls our existential reality, then what can we say about the prophets that, living under similar or worse existential circumstances before the influence of organized religions, were able to overcome those strong neuro-humoral emotional satisfaction and do the right thing where self interest was not in exclusive control of behavior? What guided their sacrificial behavior against self-interest? More to come.

SUMMARY AND CONCLUSIONS

The living human species, and to a large extent other subhuman species, share a wide spectrum of properties and phenomena that are entirely absent from inanimate matter.

Living organisms undergo metabolic activity, grow and differentiate, respond to sensory stimulation, move, develop complex, organized functional structures, show the results of inherited environmental fluctuations, reproduce and die. They also develop significant ecological adaptive fitness to changing environments. Can the rationalized metaphor of the epistemological human abstraction, be separated from the circumstantial, ontological human of our historical experience? Quare . . . This is what we find in controlled studies.

The physical aspects of their lives involves not only the replication of the nucleic acids that carry the genetic information, the memetic/epigenetic growth and maturation of the organism through a sequence of developmental steps that, exclusively in the case of humans, includes the ability to introspectively discover his individualized identity from others and the surroundings. The discovery of self coevolves with the faculty of language, now able to represent existential reality as metaphors which most likely share an embodiment with other vital neuronal networks in the brain real estate. Like other animals, inherited and environmentally-acquired servo controls guide the genetic and epigenetic preservation of biological life and its relevant neurohumoral concomitants. Unlike other animals, humans, in addition, rely on their unique ability of being self-conscious of self and others and evolve the language faculty for communication with self and others in creating a safe and progressive social environment fit for reproductive and creative social conviviality. Is the mind's conscious linguistic representation of existential reality as conceptual metaphor abstractions separate from the quotidian unconscious/subconscious servo control of behavior? Can the physical sense-phenomenal, perceptual data bases and their metaphysical metaphor representations thereof both instantiated/embodied and share common neuronal networks? If so, which one is in control in the decision-making process. Quare . . . it all depends. If we depend on recorded history we would have to conclude that by and large experiencing the satisfaction of an adapted biopsychosocial equilibrated well being at the very moment when a decision must be made will trump any other logically-based abstraction or altruistic motive. Only by exception will be found the exemplary lives of historical prophets who seem to be guided by the larger, transcendental view of the metaphor abstraction coded by the language faculty; many a times performing conscious altruistic acts contrary to self interests. Why so? Are they aliens from another galaxy, immune from the pains and tribulations of existential reality or are they privy to extrasensory information?

Lakoff, in his seminal work on 'Embodied cognition' 1963, in open defiance of Chomskian language dogma that grammar was independent of meaning, had already considered the idea that the mind is not only represented in the brain but that the physical brain is causally efficient on controlling the metaphysical mind and not the other way around! Except in the cases of the prophets. However counter-intuitive as it may sound, it is a self-evident fact of life for the majority of us mortals. To our knowledge, nobody has even tried to understand the details of this neuronal network instantiation/embodiment of language representations as universals, as metaphor virtual reflections of existential reality. Thus, to understand the meaning of life and consciousness (not robotic awareness) we must cross disciplines, both the ontological perceptual of the natural physical sciences and the epistemological conceptual of metaphysical logic and adopt a hybrid epistemontological approach because our cognition of life and existence, that precedes every decision-making act, is influenced, if not determined, by our individualized experiences in the real time physical world. In the opinion of the undersigned there may have been a basic grammar structure, a la Chomsky, that enable communication to satisfy early basic childhood needs and then became the subject of a continuous evolution guided psycho-social adaptive strategies, a type of generative semantics where much of our language structure derives from physical environmental interactions during the first few years of life. See also: Lakoff and Johnson, **'Metaphors We Live By'.**

CHAPTER 7

Theory of Everything . . .
Accessible. Anthropic Existentialism

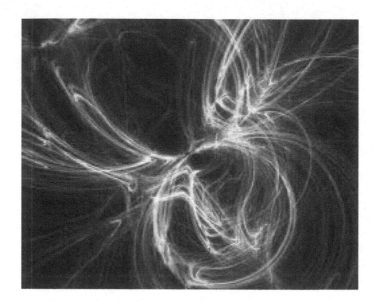

In this brief and simplistic restatement of the obvious, this represents an after-thought always lingering after reviewing any TOE model.

If we were able to consider ALL objects and events in 'de facto' current existence anywhere ('everything') as amenable to be represented or substituted by proper symbolic or sentential logic language (mathematical objects) then we can claim they belong to the 'set of all sets'. See sets.

'Ab initio', what seems like a simple linguistic statement turns into an un-surmountable contradiction. How can the 'everything' set be simultaneously a member and a non-member of itself. See Russell's paradox. So much for our human self evident limitation in perceptually accessing the structure and function of 'everything' that is, not to mention writing metaphysical logic poems about reducing 'everything' there is to mathematical formulations. If any brilliant physico-mathematical theoretician dares to bargain on a mathematical theory-poem whose axiomatic content can ALSO be contrived by an equally imaginative colleague into providing 'true' statements about its denial, then the theory is either incomplete, inconsistent, both of the above or wrong. See Gödel's incompleteness theorem. However, this is not necessarily a call to stop writing 'Theories of Everything' poems because even when a final and invariant 'reality in se' formulation may, in principle, be found, our human species cannot corroborate it other than assessing its predictive value within our short, historical, temporal sojourn on earth.

Furthermore, if we also consider that 'everything' is either contained within boundaries or dispersed 'ad infinitum' into the great nowhere, there is no doubt that, mathematically, we'd rather compose credible scientific poems on transfinities than in-accessible infinities. If so, we need set-theoretical formulations defining the topological space containing 'everything' so that relevant transfinite invisibilities may be adequately homeomorphically or homotopically represented such that their interactions, connectivities, transformations or continuities may, when present, be hopefully defined as Abelian mathematical functions. See topological space.

If we where to learn something useful to apply to real time existential reality we would have to compactify our efforts and use a metric that deals with finite objects contained inside a closed container with boundaries. But if we include 'everything' inside, e.g., a sphere (or its homeomorphic or homotopic topological equivalent) we will find that epistemologically, that portion of 'everything' outside the sphere will become a subset of 'everything' forever in-accessible to humans as to its invariant structure and function. Is this the theological subset resisting being framed into logical formulations?

As we have discussed elsewhere, when exercising our free will faculty to consent, it is that brain attractor phase space alternative that harmonizes better with ongoing biopsychosocial well being that is consented to when making a decision, notwithstanding more rational solutions available.

Physical and metaphysical determinism are ultimately unsupported beliefs in mental closure paradigms, whether in its physico-mathematical or theological varieties. As we emphasized above, there is no denying that either position satisfies the psychic needs of their adherents and, more important, either one or both may be true and we wouldn't be able to corroborate their possible invariant truth.

There is no doubt about the usefulness of evolutionary or thermodynamic theories in explaining the 'why' or 'what' of our macro reality complex systems yet their behavior is not predicated on micro-level physical laws because it emerges naturally consequent to their innate complexity. This way 'emergent' behavior may be considered a module of a 'process' philosophy subset as briefly suggested elsewhere. It should now be obvious to all the tremendous success of quantum theory not only in scientific but also in philosophical pursuits. The quasi-deterministic, probabilistic nature of its tenets and predictions, often leading to *spontaneous* mathematical chaos when initial conditions are ever so slightly changed, is in our opinion, an example of an inaccessible natural order beyond the direct reach of our perceptual and conceptual human faculties, in open violation of entropy considerations. Chaos is NOT randomness but evidence of order in a complex system. See <u>mathematical chaos</u>.

The order we humans experience in the sensory and historical domains maybe can be extrapolated to transfinity at the cosmological and sub-Planckian levels of reality. It is very tempting to write a poem on why and how the organizing role of Newtonian gravity in macro reality cannot play a similar role in sub-atomic micro-reality if we could only harmonize the 'Standard Model' relativistic and the quantum aspects of both models. Reality is one, local variations at different levels notwithstanding. While we may agree that a probabilistic quantum theoretical approach to existential reality is superior to any deterministic faith model approach because it makes room for both ontological and epistemological aspects to hybridize into a unit whole dealing with the real time probabilities and uncertainties of the mesoscopic domain of enquiry which must be, for practical purposes only, within accessible reach into representable transfinities. Leave infinities inside the esthetic domain for artists to ponder.

8 Neurons, the Mesoscopic Boundary Between Quantum and Newtonian Physics

Back to Existential Reality

Quantum Gravity

ABSTRACT

Any credible model of human brain dynamics must address the issues attending intra-species, interspecies and transfinite reciprocal information transfer. The quantum theoretical approach has been very successful in the microphysics and macrophysics levels of organization. But at the human existential, mesoscopic level, inside our 4-dimensional human Minkowsky cage, we have a long way to go for reasons we will briefly analyze below. Can we apply the same analytical and technological know-how approaches to living systems? We can identify neuronal properties that in theory may lend themselves to a quantum scrutiny, e.g., neuron micro-tubular architecture, ion channel structural design and neuronal membrane's electrical gradients.

Once more we stress the need to approach the conundrum of consciousness and universal reality by underlying the anthropic principle that sustains and gives meaning to any fact or speculation about human existential reality. It is the human brain dynamics that ultimately spell out the conditions sine qua non that are ontologically described or epistemologically explained. We are the observers and narrators of reality, a new Copernican revolution that brings man back to the center of the universe.

We consider the preceding 'back to basics' arguments as the underlying substratum on which to elaborate a submodel of consciousness resting on solid and reliable measurements whose probable meanings to living humans existence are the result of rigorously applied metaphysical logic analytical tools as the starting point. We feel that the finite and measurable living mesoscopic domain, the human brain, bridging the two opposite micro/macro transfinity domains, together form a coherent unified whole. Because of the supercomplexity of living systems, specifically of the human brain, very little work has been done on neuronal systems underlying biophysical chemistry. The time is ripe to overhaul, if necessary, those previous conceptualizations that may present a barrier to further understanding of brain dynamics, e.g., the relevance of quantum gravity in classical atomic theory. We take one brief first step by outlining the possible approaches towards that end.

INTRODUCTION

The BPS mesoscopic sub-model of brain dynamics is not necessarily herein endorsing a proposal for a universal quantum theoretical explanation applicable to all levels of organization, from the sub-Planckian micro to the cosmological macro reality, however tempting it becomes to argue that it does. Instead we need first to reconcile the natural laws governing the micro and macro domains in an effort to better understand the brain dynamics of a living brain system at the existential mesoscopic level. We have tentatively suggested elsewhere mechanisms for intraspecies information transfer[1]—essentially a modified W. Freeman's transactional model[2]—and for interspecies reciprocal communication via mirror neurons[3].

Meanwhile we continue to examine the theoretical possibility of a quantum gravity model using a putative Schwarzschild nucleus in biomolecules/atoms that we find necessary to explore for those aspects of the neuronal structural/functional cytophysiology amenable to achieve and sustain a quantum coherent state notwithstanding the immediate environmental conditions contrary to the attainment of such state, such as macromolecular size, ambient temperature and intra/extra cellular background noise among others. These we will briefly examine below in our quantum theoretical scrutiny. We are encouraged by the growing evidence of quantum behavior in biological systems and the successful application of its principles in macro systems like laser and superfluid/superconductance technology and semiconductors.[4]

ARGUMENTATION

We consider the development of computer-assisted technology a welcome explosion of facts and theoretical leads into even more, heretofore unknown, possibilities of penetrating deeper into the invisible treasures nature still holds in secret. Yet we also notice, with some regret, that many able investigators often forget that even their sense-phenomenal perceptual descriptions of objects or events are not absolute invariants, not to mention their conceptual explanations or conjectures about the invisible causal agents making the same sensory detections possible, i.e., reality is a process made possible by our living processing minds in action. This includes both our internal body-proper and external environmental sensory perceptual activity generating descriptions or scales for measurements. The problem gets more serious when conceptualizing by using language tools to explain the invisible forces or energies ostensibly controlling the observable behaviors where both internal and external, perceptual and conceptual elements are inextricably intertwined.

The most common delusional 'breakthroughs' in science that we notice is found when language representations, whether symbolic or sentential, are often confused with the actual physical object or event being abstracted into their linguistic equivalent, the proverbial confusing the map with the territory. Space and time scales are often construed to be absolute and independent physical realities instead of what they really are, i.e., convenient mathematics language tools for the consistent abstract representation of actual or inferred material objects or events as they ostensibly change their physical configuration or position, whether visible or not to our senses. To be consistent we register the observed or inferred 'change' in terms of an agreed-to abstract scale of time and space. This results in our existential 4-d space-time convenient dimensions. To further accommodate the observed repeating/recursive cycles of change we invent the imaginary or negative time, i.e., Minkowsky-Einstein 4-d space-time dimensions. This frequent confusion is specially so in particle physics as recently demonstrated when trying to identify the Higgs boson 'forces' with the powerful hadron collider at CERN. Subatomic particles or galactic black holes both owe their existence to a conscious observer's mind . . . and then only as probabilities. All of reality, whether sensory experienced or mentally conceptualized . . . .   or not, exists because a living creature witnessed its presence and his conscious effort 'created' it, as it were. Matter, however small its subdivision in microreality or large its aggregation in the macro level, has attributions, e.g., dimensions, configurations, position, shapes, colors, etc. Attributes do not have an independent invariant existence from the material entity it describes. Life seems the common independent denominator that makes reality possible. This is not to say that, for the first human being born, all of sense-phenomenal macro reality came into sudden existence as a function of his evolving state of consciousness, it was already there. All we can do is look into the deeper skies, and assume you are looking into a past that was but survives for our conceptual scrutiny and write erudite poetry about how things probably were as revealed to our limited human observers. Like we said before: ". . . we are forced to consider not just the fleeting moment we call present, the 'being', as it evolves or 'becomes' past in transit into a potential future, but also to predict with variable degrees of certainty its evolution into that future, the 'becoming' we may control . . ." Consequently, we had also summarized the uncertainty as: "We can no longer say that the past has been but is no longer, while the future will come to be but is not yet."

An additional level of complexity springs forth when we realize that the human species survival depends on social conviviality through the aegis of verbal and non-verbal interspecies exchange of survival data as we discussed elsewhere. It may well be that the sense-phenomenal experience of individuals gets merged into a 'survival social reality" of sorts, a world of cooperating conscious agents trying to fashion a biopsychosocial model of species survival taking into consideration all relevant finite ontological and transfinite epistemological aspects of 'reality' as we have suggested before.

Another aspect of brain dynamics that seems to elude the current investigators of mind/brain phenomena is the fundamental role theology plays in the real life of human beings as witnessed by history. All humans believe because not all important and relevant aspects of reality are self-evident by sensory detection or immediate logical inference. All humans seem to experience the psychosocial need to explain their origins and destinies. Science and religion are meant to be two different domains of our species mental activity because they serve different purposes in the biopsychosocial economy of the human species yet they interact synergistically to provide the tools to conquer and control the physical environmental habitat on the one hand and the moral and ethical survival tools of psychosocial conviviality in the environmental niche. This has been amply discussed and elaborated on in many previous articles by the undersigned.[7]

It should seem clear to anyone watchful enough to have 'experienced' those relevant invisible forces in nature that significantly affect our existence, that we cannot rely exclusively on our limited perceptual sensory information bank to configure our model of reality. We must also depend on our ability to conceptualize those experienced and vital invisible energies/forces present and harmonize both into an indelible hybrid whole—an epistemontological hybrid—the best we can within the un-aided reaches of our also very limited brain combinatorial resources when compared to computer processing resolution.

When we represent those significant invisible forces or energies influencing our existence by applying the mathematical logic languages available, it often creates the delusion in the observer of mastering the invariant and absolute configuration of the physical essence/matter those descriptive or explanatory attributes belong to. But we should know better. Wisdom is to us more properly the informed mental act of tentatively accepting the Cartesian doubt as a guiding tool for discovery as we journey along the path through existence with a commitment to an open-mindedness able to include—or exclude—whatever constitutive element,—genetic or memetic, perceptually sensed or conceptually inferred, internal body proper or external—that is instrumental in positively influencing our adaptive, quotidian, decision-making process; all within the context of our real-time, ongoing and individualized biopsychosocial reality.

It also seems clear, as human recorded history shows, that perceptual and conceptual reality evolve in cycles of recursive spiral gyrations where 'the more things change, the more they remain the same' within our species life span as registered for the macro systems interactivity. Yet invisible and significant micro system changes loom unregistered as yet, waiting to be discovered and identified.

Then we are ready to marry the Newtonian macro reality with the quantum micro reality into a unified hybrid whole. Otherwise the perceptual information on macro systems commits many gifted individuals to a blind faith in evolution by natural selection,—the clever, credible Darwinian type—as the exclusive mechanism underlying change. Yet, these very same Darwinian religionists, although also committed to a scientific methodology approach in their conclusions seem to ignore that natural laws predict that systems would inexorably evolve towards their lowest free energy state, by definition, the lowest possible level of organization. This would be, ab initio, logically inconsistent with the obvious **spontaneous** organization of the ordered natural systems we daily observe or otherwise infer as we witness them at practically all levels of micro/macro reality.

This makes Watson's 'Enformed Theory' claim for a pre-existing fundamental negentropic drive for systems to **spontaneously** self-organize in nature as being inconsistent with natural laws as we currently understand and interpret them. Life and consciousness are not, by applying the rules of scientific methodology, the **spontaneous** consequence of the activity of a pre-existing, uncaused 'enformed' system. We rather suspect instead it is the result of the conceptual elaboration of a living self-conscious human being and thereby awaiting evaluation as to its predictive value to real-time humans in their 4-d space-time habitat. Matter has characteristic attributions that define its degree of structural and functional complexity and the eventual attainment of such cannot be logically attributed to a non-material causal agent unless enformism joins the credo of the theological club of believers. Life and self-consciousness, as we know them, are far from being adequately described or explained by enformism's brilliant fictional poetry. Robotic **awareness** of environmental variables, sophisticated and complex as a human being can program them to be, is a far cry from **self-consciousness** ability to distinguished self from others as we have explained elsewhere so many times. A sophisticated thermostat can respond to (become aware of) a critical temperature level by executing the most complex adjustments imaginable except being self conscious of its own participation.

The mesoscopic level is defined, for the purpose of this brief discussion, as: a sub-discipline of <u>condensed matter physics</u> dealing with materials the size of a <u>molecule</u> measuring in the range of micrometers (range of bacteria or viruses). This level of organization may represent the boundary between the newtonian macroscopic and the quantum microscopic domains that need to be reconciled. It would seem like e.g., an aggregation of microscopic quantum sub atomic particles until it attains the mesoscopic level of sugar, phosphates or nucleic acids leading to macroscopic DNA polymers in a brain structure should not have a fragmented theoretical structure/function explanation.

A familiar example is illustrated when, e.g., current travels continuously along a **wire as its diameter increases according to classical physics but in discrete steps (quantized) along increasing mesoscopic diameters, as observed in conductance through nano-scale devices where surface accumulation of atoms/electrons is greater. These differences are due to quantum confinement (circular quantum dots) and shows up when the diameter of the particle approximates the magnitude of the <u>wavelength</u> of the electron's <u>wave function</u>. Impurities along a mesoscopic conducting surface may also bring about 'random' oscillations in the form of disturbing experimental fluctuations during measurements of brain electrical activity. This is due to intra/inter neuronal oscillatory activity. These may be caused by **microscopic** neuronal sub-threshold variations in membrane potential, **mesoscopic** local field variations in wave amplitude due to constructive/destructive wave interference seen in EEG or MEG or **macroscopic** interacting, feedback action potentials in neuronal ensembles, (e.g., field potentials in delta or theta activity) respectively, all of which can be recorded in EEG or MEG. Neural oscillations are still far from being understood but brain imaging techniques are making it easier to analyze.

The paradox of having macromolecules whose structural and functional attributes are controlled by their constituent micro particles, yet require different analytical /mathematical models for the macro (classical physics) and micro (quantum physics) components is mind-boggling. One suspects that some of the bosonic particle dimensions are below the Schwartzchild radius introducing dark matter (micro black holes) issues not taken into consideration by current atomic theory. Unfortunately we are not able yet to justify the existence of weakly interacting bosons giving rise to equivalent BEC condensates at human body temperatures and thereby demonstrate how their quantum effects can be measured/observed on a **macroscopic scale. The problem of preventing the decoherent molecular collapse under the noisy thermal background remains unsolved. Once this stabilization problem is resolved experimentally we can successfully apply the Schrodinger analytical equations at any level of particle organization. How will anyone apply quantum statistics at the mesoscopic scale is anybody's guess. Fortunately there are well studied systems, e.g., electron transfer particle (ETP) in photosynthesis or ion transfer through protein channels in membranes, that can be used to test these ideas. Maybe all that is required is a transient state of quantum **coherence to overcome the disrupting effects of thermal noise. This transient state may result from the sudden acceleration of ions across membrane channels generating a positive vortex of magnetic flow and the corresponding negative vortex of electric flow. At this point it may be worthwhile to recall from the exposition above that we are talking about

particle flows, whatever their dimensions; charge or magnetism or whatever other relevant **attributes** that do not have an independent existence.

SUMMARY AND CONCLUSIONS

The completion of the mesoscopic domain characterization depends on a previous successful reconciliation of the models for quantum microscopic and classic macroscopic physical laws. By intuition we feel that the problems surrounding the apparent difficulties in reconciling classical physics (general relativity) and quantum physics is centered around the issue of quantum gravity and gravitons because of either conceptual mis-apprehensions and/or experimental failures of the super hadron colliders to detect gravitons or Higgs bosons. Both gravitons' existence remains a mystery. Conceptually it makes no sense in considering gravitons as "massless particles" which sounds like a "mass-less mass" contradiction just because it's 'mass' is beyond measurable detection and, more important, because it may exist at dimensions below the critical Schwarzschild radius where the gravitational effects of condensed matter micro black holes cannot be ignored and may forever change the organization of the classical periodic table to accommodate heretofore unknown particle association by non-classical chemical bonding. It may well be that we can no longer ignore that **important fourth fundamental interaction of quantum gravity in the formation of molecular chemical bonds. Reconciling quantum theory with <u>general relativity</u> will bring all known <u>fundamental interactions</u> under same umbrella model encompassing micro, meso and macro scales, a truly Theory of Everything. The problem of reconciling the convenient coordinate systems we humans have invented when describing dimensional differences in space (<u>frame of reference</u>.) is a task for pure mathematician theorists to solve in the search for that lofty goal of diffeomorphism, i.e., <u>invariance</u> in the formulation of the appropriate physical laws valid for small or large distance scales, at all Euclidian and non-Euclidian dimensional mindscape levels. This means, among other things, a reduction of all that <u>multi-dimensional array</u> of significant variables inside our 4-d Minkowsky cage to manageable symbolic representations, more likely as a second rank <u>tensor</u> at high energies where gravitational forces remain thus far <u>nonrenormalizable</u>. If successful, like investigators did when tackling the complexity of the <u>infinite</u> integrals of <u>perturbation theory</u> in <u>quantum electrodynamics</u>. Are we then ready for a new atomic theory of matter?

At that time, as quoted elsewhere, "From the many sense-phenomenal objects and/or events in our immediate environment (including memories) only a limited number of steady states of discrete, individualized neuronal patterns (attractor basins) are set-up to respond exclusively to particular stimuli in the future.

These would activate a particular set of bulbar neurons acting as a relay switch to a corresponding attractor basin uniquely coupled to different memory, emotional and physiological pattern of responses (mental state). When these signals were analyzed on the oscilloscope screen they were found to resemble chaotic systems with 'attractor basins'. Once it was experimentally documented that there is a probabilistic nature to brain dynamics . . . ," and we add, all consistent with a new variety of 'free will by consent'. This way, at the mesoscopic level of existential reality ". . . . we are forced to consider not just the fleeting moment we call present, the 'being', as it evolves or 'becomes' past in transit into a potential future, but also to predict with variable degrees of certainty its evolution into that future, the 'becoming' we may control: and free will to choose from available 'futures scenarios'. In so doing we acknowledge an involuntary shift away from the reductionist physical approach into the metaphysical 'emergence' realm of 'process' philosophy . . . . in explaining day to day to day changes, including cerebral plasticity, an emergent phenomenon they call the attractor hypothesis" To make things more manageable our BPS model has tried to concentrate on brain sinks at pre-motor brain cortex that are in constant renewal (dynamic plasticity) and concentrating related information ready to be freely chosen by consent after taking into consideration the ongoing emotional state of the subject/actor.

Reconciling Quantum Physics and General Relativity Theory

An Argument for the Dark Baryonic DNA/RNA Premise

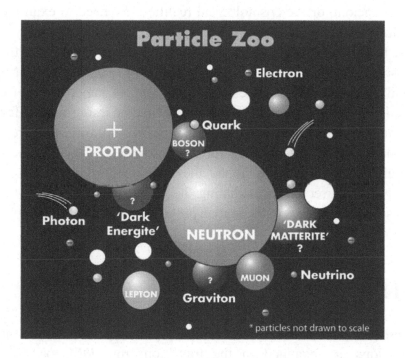

INTRODUCTION

Quantum Field Theory (QFT) is the mathematical and conceptual framework for contemporary elementary particle physics trying to answer what the fundamental characteristics of the material world are, such as, is existential reality—perceptually observed or conceptually inferred reality—constantly changing or are there certain permanent features? What is basic and what is merely a matter of perspective and appearance? What are the fundamental features of matter, whether measured or inferred, and its interactions? How is the current mathematical structure of either competing explanation interfering with the objective analysis on the creation and annihilation of "particles" like electrons and photons?

QFT, an extension of <u>quantum mechanics</u> (QM), is relativistically invariant and has been a success story for more than half a century by narrowing its scope of intervention to explain the interactions between charged particles and the electromagnetic field in quantum electro-dynamic theory (QED). This, as opposed to QM with an equally successful history as a quasi-scientific probabilistic tool reflecting the inherent sensory and brain combinatorial limitations of the human observer, contrary to the observer independence of QFT better suited for philosophical speculation. Yet, it has been very successful empirically, notwithstanding its metaphysical implications at variance with the central classical dogma of particulate matter—sensory detected or inferred—and its circumstantial manifestations to the observer such as its propagation as waves (de Broglies wavicles) in fields, its sensory color detection or its inferred particulate presence outside the visible spectrum depending on its frequency detection. Reality is one, whether we detect particles within the ontological domain of measurements or the epistemological domain of the kind of speculation controlled by metaphysical logic of probabilities of structural and functional dynamics at the invisible level of the sub-Planckian or the cosmological realities. We need to examine the adequacy of the standard dimensional formulation structure used e.g., the string theory unidimensional line or loop, the bidimensional plane—straight or curved—of relativistic theory, the static tridimensional space or the dynamic quadrimensional space-time of Minkowsky, the multidimensional space-time of symmetric or spin-coupled super symmetric models, etc. and then reconcile them mathematically as one all encompassing reality formulation, i.e., as one free from observer-dependent manifestations. To follow here are some selected examples, non-mathematically expressed for my convenience ☺ and that of most of the non-mathematical guru readers. It is hoped these arguments will make the existence of dark baryonic DNA/RNA receptors mediating the reciprocal information transfer between transfinity and a suitable acceptor in the human pre-motor cortical attractor phase space more credible as a premise.

ARGUMENTS

Reconciling quantum physics and general relativity theory. For starters, the ontologically relevant formulations are changed in the transition from QM to QFT mathematical representations because, as suggested earlier, the wave function values in QM are influenced by measurements and 'operators' which subsequently influence the quantum field identification of space of states, i.e., like a second quantization has virtually taken place and by magic now quantum fields paradoxically become 'theoretically-inferred observables'! Only **true** <u>observables</u>, not quantum fields, should be represented by linear operators, e.g., the case of the Klein-Gordon equation when a **measured** position and/or momentum is conveniently represented by the corresponding quantum mechanical operator(s). Consequently, the operator valued field $\varphi(\mathbf{x},t)$ in QFT is *not* analogous to the wave function $\psi(\mathbf{x},t)$ in QM, i.e., is a misrepresentation—by mathematical manipulation—of an observable reality, i.e., this results in a smeared field $\varphi(f) = \int \varphi(x)f(x)dx$ with supp(f) ⊂ O, where supp(f) is the support of the test function f and O is a bounded open region in Minkowski space-time.

And we ask, which in reality are states and which are measurable quantities? States, as opposed to observables, are abstract entities with no immediate spatio-temporal meaning.

The confusion comes about when the standard model of elementary particle physics is restricted from its **universal** reach to the **narrower scope** of a particular energy domain range by being considered as an effective field theory (EFTs) explaining the probable changes within the range of energy under analysis. No doubt, imho, that when dealing with our real time existential dynamics at the mesoscopic level we are better off with this narrowing of scope to lower energy levels by eliminating the irrelevant infinities by the convenient procedure of renormalization. The problem is that this convenient restriction may isolate our intended explanation about relevant higher/lower energy interactive influences present. Intuitively, one wonders why should there be one physics theory explaining the invisible but influential micro sub Planckian and a different one for the equally relevant and invisible cosmological domain? And we keep asking, why not one last fundamental theory incorporating these two micro/macro invisibilities into a realistic mesoscopic epistemontological hybrid? Or, have we reached the limits of our human species brain combinatorial capacities? Are we ever going to hybridize QFT and general relativity theory into an evolving mesoscopic, real time, working, epistemontological unified theory of ALL measurable natural forces and logically inferred invisible forces, including gravitation?

One of the complex unresolved problems has been, e.g., how can the conveniences of a specific mesoscopic energy range under QFT analysis incorporate the Planck scale energy level force of gravitation as a relevant dark baryonic DNA/RNA energy without the theoretical assumption of point-like interactions inevitably leading to intractable infinities? My suggestion, going way back to the early Greek atomistic thinking, is that there are only particles as fundamental objects and their corresponding dynamic attributions (e.g., energy, propagation mode, size/shape configuration, etc.), measurable or not. Leave it to theology to explain particles origins and destination and if it makes you happier, assume the particles entered into our existential lives as the result of the immediate post Big Bang expansion/ cooling crystallization leading to the formation of evolving fermions, bosons, quarks, BEC condensates, etc., not bad poetry! ☺

Intuitively, IMO, adimensional point singularities may be better considered as unit Einstenian energetic particles beyond our experimental human capacities to objectively describe their dimension or mass by observation. We can develop this poem further by conveniently representing the vacuum unit mass/energy by a unit Planck dimension (a Dirac string?) to include gravity (thereby avoiding 'infinities'). This should conveniently also extend its radius of locality action by invoking its ability to vibrate at convenient frequencies, reaching beyond the energy restrictions of QFT. Thus the string can be straight, curved or loop shaped but, more important, strings can now reach and reciprocally interact and influence other particles on an extended distance beyond the 10^{-33} centimeters of Planck's unit length. Now, at the mesoscopic level of interest, strings 'become' quantum particles with convenient quantum numbers assigned in harmony with their vibrational frequency/energy

and equivalent Einstenian mass. Consequently, a dynamic particle-based premise implying a dimensional, temporal changing volume, measurable or inferred, e.g., a Minkowsky 4-d spacetime arrangement need not necessarily imply the hard-to-conceptualize 'compactified unidimensional state' with $10 \rightarrow 26$ dimensions plus the coordinates values where to find the unavoidable particulate matter in order to explain their invisibility to experimental detection. Furthermore one cannot accept as an 'observable' claims of experimental knowledge about measurable quantities such as charge, energy or momentum of a particle in a field that refer to infinitely extended regions of space-time formally requiring measurements to take place in the whole universe! We sorely need a consistent algebraic reformulation of true observables in QFT to be taken as the basic entities in the mathematical formulation of quantum physics, one that is compatible with the Hilbert space formulation. This approach should hopefully provide the element of **locality** restricting true observables to finite space-time regions.

The dynamic interaction of elementary particles require tracking their symmetry transformations in the properties of particles/quantum fields which are conserved or broken if the symmetry is varying during the reciprocal information transfer. The linear translational momentum or rotational angular momentum invariance of a system defines a conservation law. We need not consider now inner transformations such as so-called gauge transformations relating to yet more abstract properties. The explanatory power of <u>symmetry and symmetry breaking</u> is fundamental to understand the continuous reciprocal information exchange between transfinity and the human neocortical attractor phase space mediated by our dark baryonic DNA/RNA receptor. Fortunately the present theories of elementary particle interactions can be understood by deduction from general principles.

Symmetries are not only defined for Lagrangians but they can also be found in empirical data and phenomenological descriptions. Symmetries can thus bridge the gap between descriptions which are close to empirical results ('phenomenology') and the more abstract general theory which is a most important reason for their heuristic force.

SUMMARY AND CONCLUSIONS

The first one is that quantities like.eg., total charge, total energy or total momentum of a field are unobservable since their measurement would have to take place in the whole universe. Accordingly, quantities which refer to infinitely extended regions of space-time should not appear among the observables of the theory as they do in the standard formulation of QFT. The mathematical aspect of the problem is that a field at a point, $\varphi(x)$, is not an operator in a Hilbert space. The practical physical counterpart of the problem is that it would require an infinite amount of energy to measure a field at a point of spacetime.

A true reconciliation of quantum physics and relativity theory is a tall order and may require the algebraic approach to demonstrate that the experimental data for QFT is limited to space-time **localization** properties of particulate matter from which **other** relevant properties should not be inferred. The Stern-Gerlach experiment is an illustration of this limitation in getting space-time distributions of some dots of detected particles originating from a particle source striking a sensitive photographic plate. Mathematicians need to work out how may Heisenberg's matrix mechanics and Schrödinger's wave mechanics can incorporate algebraic geometry, all performing inside Hilbert space with the same abstract structure. This way, we hope, the transient existence of functional magnetic monopoles controlling the reciprocal magnetic flux of information between source and destination across a DNA/RNA quantum computer of sorts may not be so mysterious.

Athens Raphael

INTRODUCTION

How does the functionally-limited human brain get a functional handle in describing or explaining an important and relevant object or event when the brain's cognition is conditioned on the probability of the perceptually-verified occurrence of the act (which itself is predicated upon the perspective of the observer in relation to the observed), not to mention the unavoidable, ever present biases? Quantum theory has successfully hybridized the perceptually verified and the conceptually logical aspects derived from the observation thanks to the **Standard Model** of <u>particle physics</u> theory modeling the interactions between the <u>electromagnetic</u>, <u>weak</u>, and <u>strong</u> nuclear forces that mediate the measured and/or logically inferred dynamics of the known subatomic particles. However, it is incomplete in having ignored the required incorporation of the perspective/relativistic aspect and thus falls short of being a complete theory of fundamental interactions. It needs to be reconciled with the physics of general relativity, so that gravitation, dark energy and dark matter become part and parcel of the new unified approach encompassing the micro, meso and macro dimensions of existential reality. Perhaps new logical premises need be considered to reduce the incredibility of, e.g., 'zero-dimensional singularity point energy' sources, zero mass photons, etc. as discussed in Part I, not to mention the inconsistencies of puzzles like the strong CP problem and the hierarchy problem. This way we can make a case for quantum gravity, magnetic fluxes, axions, etc. as the credible constituents of the bridging pathways for the reciprocal information transfer between the human neocortex and transfinity as mediated by light, bosonic, dark baryonic DNA/RNA receptor as argued elsewhere. Fast, hyper linked access to Wikipedia has been provided in substitution of the classical article references.

ARGUMENTS

Before we proceed with this brief analysis we need to distinguish between the weak interaction and the strong nuclear force in operation which, alongside electromagnetism, and gravity, constitute the four fundamental forces of nature comprising the discipline of particle physics. Weak interactions are responsible for the radioactive decay of subatomic particles affecting all known fermions; that is, particles whose spin (a property of all particles) is a half-integer. Strong nuclear forces binds nucleons (protons and neutrons) together to form the nucleus of an atom and it is also the force (carried by gluons) that holds quarks together to form protons, neutrons and other hadron particles. The **weak** interaction is **unique** in that it can also break parity-symmetry and CP-symmetry (quark flavor changing), i.e., allowing quarks to swap their 'flavor' from one to another out of six available options. On the other hand the strong interaction force is about 100 times stronger than electromagnetism, which in turn is orders of magnitude stronger than the weak force interaction and gravitation.

However, gluons interact with quarks, antiquarks and other gluons because they all carry a type of charge called "color charge." This generates a 'residual force' of three types, each with a different profile and different rules of behavior, as detailed in quantum chromodynamics (QCD), the theory of quark-gluon interactions. The residual strong force thus becomes a minor residuum of the strong force which binds quarks together into protons and neutrons. The resulting force acting *between* neutrons and protons is now much weaker, because it becomes mostly neutralized *within* themselves. This is equivalent to the much weaker electromagnetic forces existing between neutral atoms (van der Waals forces) than the EM forces holding the individual atoms internally together. It would help to remember that atoms and subatomic particles have tiny magnetic fields, as in the Bohr model of an atom where even electrons display as they orbit the nucleus. Their constant motion gives rise to an associated magnetic field and, arguably, behave then as functional 'monopoles'. On the other hand permanent magnets have measurable magnetic fields because the atoms and molecules in them are arranged in such a way that their individual magnetic fields align, combining to form large aggregate fields. In particle physics, **proton decay** is a hypothetical form of radioactive decay in which the proton decays into lighter subatomic particles, such as a neutral pion and a positron. There is currently no experimental evidence that either Higgs bosons exist or proton decay occurs. Because of the **weak** interaction, a break in parity-symmetry and CP-symmetry (underline quark flavor changing) can spontaneously occur or be induced by transfinity cosmic/photon radiation at the level of the hydrogen atom in the polynucleotide.

The success of the premise invoking the presence of 'dark baryonic DNA/RNA' receptor site in the human species depends, among other things, on establishing the presence of 'quantum gravity', however transiently, responsible for the reciprocal information transfer between transfinity and the human premotor cortical attractor phase space. The information exchange across the gravitational field is likely mediated by an elementary particle of charge=0 and spin=0 to resolve the strong CP problem in quantum chromodynamics (QCD). We had previously suggested the **axion** (mass=10^{-6} to 1 eV/c^2) as such hypothetical particle, as a possible component of cold dark matter in 'dark baryonic DNA/RNA' fitting into a credible spatiotemporal structure at the sub-Planckian scale level, as argued in Part I of this discussion.

Now we expand further on these possibilities, especially at what appears to be an inconsistency between the conservation of charge conjugation (C) and parity (P) at the micro and cosmological levels of organization, always keeping our focus at the mesoscopic level of the existential real time dimension we can measure. And we ask: Why should QCD theory allow the non-trivial violation of charge conjugation and parity symmetry (CP)? Who or what causes it, how does it happen, what consequences may it eventually carry in the evolutionary path of our human species biological, psychic and social profiles that guarantee life and self-conscious free will?

Within the context of a hybrid epistemontological approach, our BPS model realizes that the empirical testing of quantum gravity as such, along standard lines, is experimentally a near-impossibility. However, the self-evident presence of a phenomenally invisible object/event does not negate its existence in the physical, but extrasensory perceptual, realm of reality. Especially when mathematical logic may provide the epistemological tool that makes it possible to unify the classical general relativity and quantum physics into a coherent micro/cosmological spatiotemporal structural whole. It would be a tall order for mathematicians to bring together the classical Einstenian relativistic velocity of light (c), the Newtonian constant (G) and the quantum physics Planck's constant (h) to express the unifying concepts of mass (m), dimensions (l) and change (t). It may also harmonize gravitational and electromagnetic (em) phenomena.

As discussed in Part I, above, our first premise is the mass/particulate basis of mesoscopic reality regardless of our experimental capacity to measure invisible dimensions such as the axion mass. There are particles and their color, shape, etc., attributions never capable of an independent existence from each other. A spherical or vortex shape, etc., without a particle is an abstract **representation** of, e.g., a particle motion! We need not identify their material origin and destiny, leaving that to theosophy speculation. We had also chosen, for simplicity, the hydrogen atom nucleus in dark baryonic DNA/RNA as the relevant particle on which to develop the sub-model of reciprocal information transfer.

It is precisely the imputed CP violation arising from QCD, however tiny and transient, what brings bosonic axions in the hydrogen **neutron** into the picture. Why assume that quarks in the standard model are massless just because they cannot be observed, especially when the existing experimental evidence strongly suggests that all of the quarks are particulate matter and consequently the strong CP problem persists. What is there to prevent the neutron—an electrically neutral particle—from experiencing an intrinsic charge separation and thus violating CP? Yet, it may be easier to visualize the infinitesimally small CP violating interactions as originating from QCD induced **functional** monopoles in protons instead of in the large electric dipole moment for the neutron. Remember that functionally both poles are independently engaged in different reciprocal processing activities and as such transiently behaving as functional gravitational monopoles across the magnetic flux path even though structurally they are geometric dipoles, i.e., serving as an intracranial connecting bridge between the dark baryonic DNA/RNA receptor site and the pre-motor neocortical attractor phase space. Somehow the global supersymmetry (Peccei-Quinn symmetry?) becomes spontaneously (or induced?) broken and transiently producing the light bosonic axion particles that will now allow the transfer of information carried by particulate gravitons(?) This way photons traveling to and from transfinity could interact with the gravitational field to become virtual or real axions and amplified by the cycling back and forth through the magnetic/gravitational field many times, as needed. The conversions of axions to photons and vice versa in **strong** electromagnetic fields at the cosmological level (Primakoff effect) is actively being investigated and can be produced, e.g., when X-rays scatter off electrons and protons in the presence of **strong** electric fields. Other fermionic dark matter candidates like WIMPs and MACHOs should also be investigated at both cosmologic and micro levels of organization.

SUMMARY AND CONCLUSIONS

How may the H atom of polynucleotides may be the target of transfinite radiation and/or the object of spontaneously induced nuclear baryonic transformations leading to changes in charge and parity (CP) as predicted by the nuclear weak and strong forces in operation?

According to the Standard Model, gauge bosons are defined as force carriers (F) that mediate the strong, weak, and electromagnetic fundamental interactions and F= **mass** x acceleration.

The bosons of the Standard Model all have spin—like all matter particles—and their value is 1. Consequently these will not follow the spin-statistics theorem and the Pauli exclusion principle that constrain the underline{spin $\frac{1}{2}$ fermions}, e.g., photons, and for that reason do not have a theoretical limit on their spatial density (number per volume). The type of boson we are interested is part of the composite particles (hadrons) containing not a quark and an antiquark (mesons), but **three quarks** (baryons). Of these, the proton and the neutron are the two baryons having the smallest mass from the smallest atom, hydrogen. Because quarks carry electric charge and weak isospin they will interact with other fermions both electromagnetically and via the weak interaction. We have also chosen first generation baryonic particles of unit mass (immediately following Big Bang) because these charged particles do not decay, as found in all atoms consisting of electrons orbiting atomic nuclei ultimately constituted of up and down quarks. But quarks can also carry color charge, and hence, interact via the strong interaction to produce a phenomenon called color confinement that results in quarks being perpetually bound to one another as composite particles (hadrons).

If we somehow could transiently gain control by cancelling the electromagnetic interactions resulting from the electric and magnetic fields then the persisting gravitation will allow particles with mass to attract one another across the gravitational flux path in accordance with Einstein's theory of general relativity and thus allowing the coexistence of both quantum theory and general relativity at least at the mesoscopic portion of the macroscopic level. This way it may arguably become unnecessary to resort to perturbation theory or the path integral formulation as approximations. It could well be that the vacuum state, and the not-so-virtual transfinity 'particle'/radiation is controlled by induced reversible absorption—back and forth—into their vacuum state? As we know Photons mediate the electromagnetic force between electrically charged particles. But in our submodel the photon is not massless as described by classical quantum electrodynamics and furthermore, the electric dipole responsible for the structuring of the EM field may not exist functionally if either pole is independently engaged in information processing, as explained. It is also relevant to remember the dynamic role of the electron who can be either a fermion or a boson according to electroweak theory. If mathematically reconciled, quantum field theory can coexist with gravitational fields and need not breakdown at the meso and/or sub-Planckian level. The controversial premise of existing bosonic, light dark baryonic polynucleotides, super symmetry, axions and a graviton may well be a worthwhile investment effort. If reconciled, it may bring us closer to an understanding of human life and conscious free will beyond the intellectual constraints inside the strait jackets of materialistic orthodoxy.

The Maxwell's equations of electromagnetism relate the electric and magnetic fields to each other and to the motions of electric charges. The standard equations provide for electric charges, and assume the non-existence of magnetic charges. If non—existing, the new terms in Maxwell's equations are all zero, and the extended equations reduce to the conventional equations of electromagnetism such as $\nabla \cdot \mathbf{B} = 0$. ($\nabla$ is divergence and $\mathbf{B}$ is the underline{magnetic $\mathbf{B}$ field}). Symmetric Maxwell's equations can be written when all charges and electric currents) are zero, the way the electromagnetic wave equation is derived. Full symmetry can be achieved if one allows for the possibility of a "magnetic charge" and a "magnetic current density" variable in the equations. Yet, we need to explain why the magnetic charge always seems to be zero?" Quantum chromodynamics (QCD) defines the interactions between quarks and gluons, with SU(3) symmetry.

This admittedly amateurish and somewhat pedantic effort at reconciling two different approaches to the same real time, 4-d existential reality is not to be construed as a new quantum gravity theory, "shoemaker . . . to your shoes", but only a red flag to any other obsessive compulsive retiree afflicted with the 'sane psychosis' of curiosity. We may have to wait for the results of the CERN hadron collider verdict on the Higgs mechanism and the hierarchy problem as it applies to quantum gravity at the mesoscopic weak energy scales before we update the Planck scale issues of the Standard Model.

In particle physics, **proton decay** is a hypothetical form of radioactive decay in which the proton decays into lighter subatomic particles, such as a neutral pion and a positron.[1] There is currently no experimental evidence that proton decay occurs.

Our preference for the baryonic proton in the hydrogen atom is that in the Standard Model, they are theoretically stable because baryon number (quark number) is conserved under normal conditions. They will not decay into other particles on their own, because they are the lightest, least energetic baryon. During the 'event horizon' immediately following the Big Bang there was symmetry breaking that favored the creation of normal baryonic matter (as opposed to antimatter) due to the rapid expansion leading to the crystallization that made possible nucleosynthetic activity. Under certain conditions (radiation induced or spontaneously) protons may undergo decay into a positron and a neutral pion that itself immediately decays into 2 gamma ray photons:

$$p+ \rightarrow e\pm + \pi 0$$

$$\pi 0 \rightarrow 2\gamma$$

While this effect would also be seen in neutrons bound inside atomic nuclei, in the case of the hydrogen atom we would only consider free neutrons known to decay into protons (plus an electron and an antineutrino) in a process called beta decay. These free neutrons have a half-life of about 10 minutes due to the weak interaction. Besides, neutrons bound inside a nucleus have, like protons, a much longer half-life ca. 10^{34} years depending on the type of decay they experience.

In quantum gravity, we posit a **virtual micro** black hole that transiently exists as a result of a quantum fluctuation of spacetime. It represents the gravitational analog of the virtual electron-positron pairs found in quantum electrodynamics. Theoretical arguments suggest that virtual black holes should have mass on the order of the Planck mass, lifetime around the Planck time, and occur with a number density of approximately one per Planck volume, all of which helps to achieve the intended harmony between quantum physics and general relativity. Furthermore if these virtual micro black holes exist, they would provide a mechanism for proton decay because when its mass increases (mass falling into the hole) it can then decrease again when Hawking radiation is emitted from the hole. This way a transformation takes effect when the particles emitted are different from those that fell in, e.g., if two of a hydrogen proton's constituent quarks fall into a virtual black hole, it is possible for an antiquark and a lepton to emerge, thus violating conservation of baryon number. Notice that by this process the black hole information loss paradox is no longer so, instead it may well constitute the basis of an evolutionary information change without any disruption of ongoing physical processes. Under these circumstances the Schwarzschild solution applies for a spherically symmetric non-rotating uncharged massive object, like an axion. For radial distances exceeding the Schwarzschild radius, the accelerations between the poles of a gravitational field are those predicted by Newton's theory of gravity and Einstein's general relativity.

We have not discussed the possible decay of protons into other subatomic particles or their radioactive decay that accompanies their ejection from the nucleus by *Proton emission*. Neither have we discuss how 'quantization' may be the result of the electron returning to the same point after the full trip around the nuclear equator, the so called phase **exp**($i\varphi$) of its wave function assumed to be unchanged, justifying the phase φ added to the wave function being the multiples of 2π.

CHAPTER

The Sane Psychosis of Curiosity. Epilogue for Truth Value

These farewell notes are meant to briefly question what roles emotional mental states may play, if any, on your ability to dig deep into the abstract representational world in search of ideas to correlate with the situation being analyzed and identify the best alternatives to choose from. I tried to outline and discuss this issue in the last two chapters of my Volume III. I had been enormously stressed by family problems. My dear ex-wife Judy was not improving after her breast cancer had come back with a vengeance. I was getting ready to donate a kidney to my older son. My youngest daughter was having family problems and my oldest daughter left our house in Deltona to join her sister in North Carolina. I had to get my mind busy to avoid being mentally crushed by my own emotional feelings. Deep concentration isolates you temporarily from your existential problems. Besides which, I had been for some time preparing for retirement from academia; I would spend time synthesizing my ideas on reality and consciousness. I thought I could integrate data from inherited genetic DNA memory, perceptual sensory input, acquired memetic memory, conceptual inferential input (based on language processing), and the associated emotional mind state, all into one comprehensive hybrid biopsychosocial (BPS) physical/metaphysical package. It would embrace the physical ontological and metaphysical epistemological, and fuse them together with the quasi-deterministic glue of quantum theory, leaving room for free will and a credible explanation for self-consciousness. A big project, indeed! I would leave out my Catholic religion, because I was convinced I could use the same arguments non-believers use to prove my point, and be more convincing thereby. Somehow, I had to escape the classical dogma that only the human mind, sensations, and rationality constituted the exclusive cognitive faculty. I had to find out what was in between, e.g., how the sense-phenomenal **perceptual** was coded into general neuronal network representations, expressing the universality of otherwise direct, singular objects/events immediately present in the environmental niche, and also how the **conceptual** was coded into general neuronal network representations expressing the indirect, mediate attributions, explanations about their meaning to the body economy in the BPS spectrum. The search for meaning was to be found with the aid of language and sentential or symbolic logic representations, making possible the cogeneration of self-consciousness and the associated emotional mental state, corresponding to the particular judgment. The interactivity relation between the sense-phenomenal (internal/external) input, genetic/memetic memory input, and their associated emotional mental state is critical. Ideally, each input would be dynamically and globally integrated, and the resulting package would be dynamically updated and retrieved from cortical spaces on short notice, as our adaptive judgment on a given contingency. Sensibility to the body-proper internal and the environmental external, as a bottom-up process, would now include not only sense-phenomenal interoceptors, exteroceptors, and proprioceptors but also quantum electromagnetic energy absorbers. The top-down process of understanding the meaning entailed the possible emergence of self-consciousness with the help of an inner proto-language, generated as a forerunner of language processing.

The common denominator behind all these speculations was what, in my opinion, had escaped the imagination of most of my colleagues: the realization that both the perceptual, bottom-up and the conceptual, top-down processes are severely limited in their capacity of resolution in our human species. Thus, when making judgment about optimal adaptive spatiotemporal responses to important contingencies, we can no longer have certainty about the truth-value of our input or output content or meaning, respectively; we only have probabilities. We have no choice but to satisfy that human innate curiosity about origins and destiny, and make mental representations of that micro sub-Planckian and macro cosmological invisibilities with the aid of metaphysical epistemological logic tools and cross our fingers. *Ergo*, the ontology value of an un-aided scientific methodology is complemented and supplemented by epistemology, because understanding and sensibility are both subserved by the faculty of modeling with a hybrid epistemic-ontological approach, which I had promised myself to develop. Thus, incomplete in the absolute sense, the practical reason that Kant defended must be now reinterpreted to include evolving explanations on the structure/function of the invisible, non-existential reality that includes theological and physicalist faiths. The cognitive processing undertaken by the rational faculty depends on the quality of the bottom-up information to produce the logical inferences underlying our top-down modal judgments, hopefully consistent and coherent, within the context of our biopsychosocial existential reality. And this is necessarily reflected in our evolving legal codes and constitutions. It is clear that the self-conscious affirmation of one's existence, the "I" as actor and observer, is situated at the executive vortex where all relevant perceptual/conceptual representations converge as the synthesis of the several semantic constituents of that cognition into the high-order cognitive singularity of a cortical premotor attractor space ready to be consciously chosen to activate the corresponding muscles or glands into action. How these primitive neural representations become further represented in the form of *a priori* logical constructs, assembled within the existential circumstance and ongoing mental state of the subject, and made available for free will access and choice may be outside the reach of rational tools. I anticipated much trouble examining what I consider the most crucial human cognitive faculty, that of making judgments. The most difficult will doubtless be explaining the induction or cogeneration of self-consciousness with the language faculty, and understanding the cooperative role between classical synaptic and electromagnetic quantum processing.

It is a new logical world we are all witnessing. The comfort of the quotidian existence under the Boolean world of truth or falsity and certainty has now evolved into the stressful uncertainty of a probabilistic world, where disjunctive and conditional statements always enter the decision-making process to preserve the truth-functional structure of logical reasoning. Many of us out there whose hobby is to model reality have to always keep in focus that our most serious brainstorm pronouncements are necessarily inferences on representations and never descriptions of observable reality. In the bottom-up phase, our brains represent inner and outer objects and events as inputs for linguistic processing into other types of metaphysical logic representations; the top-down outputs are only inferences representing a mediate cognition of that original object/event. Our particular judgment on a given situation, i.e., our opinion, is thereby the resultant of representations of previous representations until one final concept binds many representations, and worse, many concepts may comprise a single representation. Our judgments, far from being objective, are inferential and subjective. This is the best our species can offer in matters of cognitive certainty. Subjectivity combined with innate curiosity about our species' origin and destination makes room for beliefs and faiths, theological or not. I had much difficulty marketing this unpopular idea among non-theists. No less difficult was my attempt at developing a convincing formulation, where I had to settle for the cogeneration of language processing and self-consciousness as just a convenient explanation for invisible processes, outside my limits of corroboration regarding the details.

Marketing these concepts to multidisciplinary audiences is most difficult, especially when dealing with theoretical physicists and mathematicians, who would not accept that their physicalist constructs are in themselves "beliefs" not radically different from classical-symbolic or sentential-logic representations, leading to belief-type theological "propositions." The latter can be as fallible and uncertain as the former and, considering the intended influence in social conviviality, may be considered as subjectively necessary and sufficient defeasible/revokable propositions. Ultimately, both are the result of unconscious genetic and subconscious memetic processing of bottom-up inputs (from internal and external objects or events) into neuronal network representations, including their assignment of agreed-upon language-related label descriptions or attributions, predicated on their size, shape, color, etc., to be followed by conceptual elaborations, predicated on those or related previous representations of the same objects/events. At this level, the functional copula subject-predicate (object/event description or action, e.g., table is red, chair is moving) allows the formation of logical language rules, according to which judgments are expressed in a logical syntactic and semantic form necessary for communication in a given language. *Ergo*, both mathematically-induced propositions and theologically-induced beliefs are ultimately inferences about an invisible world, derived from the use and application of pure laws of logic, and expressed in a predicative copular format (subject-predicate, modal-conditional). Coetaneous with the modifications leading to the final structuring, according to truth-functional value considerations, a self-conscious identification with such circumstantial consideration ensues. In this respect, I took issue with Chomsky's syntactic-semantic vector in formulating sentential logic as being the opposite vector, based on the primacy of the innate primitive biological self-preservation imperative "meanings" ("intension") controlling syntax considerations, the details of which depend on the idiosyncrasies of the adopted language structure. Curiously, the actors behind the recent advances in technology have given low priority to issues only capable to be expressed in modal or conditional logic formats, especially when the brain's emotional states, resisting logical formulations, exert a causal influence on the outcome of a decision to act or not. Somehow physical theoreticians seem to conveniently ignore the inexorable presence of the real-life existentialist component (emotions) in every significant human judgment. Unfortunately, it is not so much about the legitimacy of a rational, truth-valued, unified composite of objective, meaningful, and relevant parts defining a claim about the ideal world, as much as it is about how the lonely leader with a given emotional mental state circumstance will translate into the needs of the society he/she represents vis-à-vis his/her own. The logically structured, semantically well-arranged, truth-valued judgment representing the best legal, moral, biological, psychic, and social interests of a collective is only a goal in clear controversy with the bio-psychosocial needs of the individualized components of the collective. All propositional "facts" or theological "beliefs" are of necessity inferences about the visible and invisible aspects of existential reality, life inside an epistemic-ontological hybrid reality we cannot escape from. *Ergo*, existential reality does not equate with objective reality. The former is an acceptable, subjective constraint of reality *in se*, whose absolute truth and meaningful values are only apparent. On the other hand, how accurate and "objective" can the human brain representations of objects/events be? Especially when further constrained by the imposed linguistic compositionality in which they must be expressed in both inner and reported proto-rational syntax/semantic straitjackets. "Objective judgments" thus elaborated are not to be confused with the symbolic or sentential logic truth of their representations, as materialists/physicalists would have us believe, logical consistency being a necessary but insufficient outcome. Symbolic or sentential logic representations of the invisibility of the noumenal or cosmological reality can be rationally intelligible, yet truth-valueless. Truth is a goal to be achieved as we travel the sinuous path along an evanescent asymptotic line. Consequently, we can only have opinions on the **probable value of our representations** of an invisible reality, and this is as close as we can go about knowing the truth of our reality. We can only aim at an isomorphic correspondence between the structure/function of an object/event and the symbolic/sentential logic representation as expressed in a syntactic/semantic copula we call an "intensional" explanation or opinion, not a description which we reserve for sense-phenomenal entities. This means that the brain cannot produce absolute truths, whether they be analytical (in differentiating) or synthetic (in integrating) representations before (*a priori*) or after (*a posteriori*) the empirical facts. For men and rabbits, all empirically-based, synthetic *a posteriori* judgments are the result of subconscious processing, and can, in theory, be programmed in a computer. They relate more to the guarantee of biological survival of the species, as they interact with a potentially hostile phenomenological environment with limited necessary resources. At the exclusively human level, where psychosocial considerations become part of the human species survival equation, we have to resort to brain representations of the chaos of sensations, and access an innate language faculty to classify, sort, combine, permute, and parse to extract the meaning of an otherwise atemporal, acausal, and asymmetric reality *in se*. Genetic and memetic memories of past and present provide the bottom-up input of coded representations, to evolve probable alternatives of adaptive responses to future contingencies, to be freely chosen by consent from dynamic cortical attractor spaces. In the process, both language and self-consciousness are cogenerated. The participation of the amygdala, hippocampus, thalamus, and limbic system in the formulation and synthesis of the representations (in harmony with natural law) into cortical phase spaces has to be detailed and remains a great challenge to cage into a credible formulation. The materialist/physicalist need not be challenged by a hybrid epistemic-ontological model of reality because, as Kant admonished, conceptual thoughts without perceptual meaningful content ("intensions") are empty, just as pure physical ontology without metaphysical epistemology is blind. The indelible complementary/supplementary and semantic interactivity of the perceptual and conceptual (ontological and epistemological) is essential for an existential cognitive act to take place, because neither senses can conceptualize, nor rationality can sense.

However, all human species limitations in perceptual/conceptual resolution being considered, it is fair to say that there may be conceptual meanings without rational underpinnings (intuitions) or perceptual experiences that resist expression as logical constructs (revelations). Should they be considered empty, bogus, or meaningless and denied cognitive status? Just like quantum theory, nowadays the best "scientific methodology," cannot qualify as **objectively** valid, it is nonetheless rationally intelligible about the invisibility of a sub-Planckian reality containing massless "objects!" Theological/theist experiences, though, cannot be combined with ontological measurements to generate quasi-objective valid arguments, as is the case with brain dynamics modeling. Recorded history and human experience of negentropy have validated the anthropocentric, self-referential, non-conceptual intuitions we know as religious beliefs. The Cartesian type of truth, preferred by materialists, would leave no room for scientific or religious beliefs, in that it requires the actual sense-phenomenal verification of the object/

event being precisely reduced to symbolic/sentential representations in its physical absence. Beliefs, by and large, are defeasible and subject to evolutionary modifications. Moderation requires that belief be subjectively and objectively sufficient and coherent with sets of other beliefs. In theory, propositions may be false, yet believers (theoretical physicists or mystics) can demonstrate that their conviction is operationally justified, until revoked in the lab or the social ecosystem niche. The embodied finitude of the human species condition justifies more cognitive flexibility. And this includes a consideration of the inseparability of the human emotional affect at all stages during the elaboration of a final judgment, a very difficult element to include/formulate into the equation. The judging capacities of existential human beings in their circumstantial *milieu* cannot be ignored by self-serving purists. I hope this emphasis on human existential realities is not construed as a free-willing Sartrian type of existentialism. It simply means that the formulation of Fodorian "propositional attitudes" has to emphasize sense-phenomenal content at the expense of self-serving logical format. For the purpose of communication, we need to categorize ongoing sense-phenomenal perceptions within the framework of an agreed-upon universal *a priori* referential, which will provide guiding rules for the evaluation of objective truth content, freed, when possible, from irrelevant modal or affective "non sequiturs," reminiscent of the Kantian "Categorical Imperatives" controlling the participation of fallacies and moral sins in the formulation of propositions. It may be necessary to psychologize modality in the structure of the subject-predicate copula to help identify the semantic content of a judgment. It is difficult to distinguish propositional attitudes from logic modalities. A predicate monadic logic concentrating on "intensional" content is valuable, yet insufficient for our limited purposes of a brain quantum dynamics model. We like to leave open the possibility of an interesting dualistic cooperation, mentioned in the last paragraph.

It is important to realize that, because human existential reality is in the brain, an understanding of its dynamics must start with the raw data of sense-phenomenal impressions, in the style of empiricist philosophy. These sensory impressions are limited in conveying information about the structure/function of existential reality. To compensate for ontological deficiencies in resolution, we need to complement/supplement the paucity of facts with an epistemological rationalist approach, based on credible, probable, but defeasible/revokable metasensorial facts, as found in metaphysical logic propositional representations. After all, cognitions arise not only from sensory data but also from innate genetic memories, acquired memetic memories, or a combination thereof. The epistemological component of the "hybrid" approach I am suggesting will accommodate whatever logical procedure is available that brings you the closest to an original sense-phenomenal description. This may take the cognitive format of substituting the invisible "form" for its visible "effects." This transition from a sensory "description" (what) to an inferred "explanation" (how) as an acceptable identification has two modes, in order of reliability: logical and natural supervenience between the invisible object/event X and the credible manifestation of its inferred presence by logical induction or a measurable effect Y. How does invisible X determine or relate to Y? Ideally, one can isolate X with logic but not in nature. X will causally determine Y if and only if X features are necessary and sufficient to generate Y features so that changes of form or semantic content in

Y will cause corresponding changes in X. In brain dynamics studies, we have only a limited number of ways of establishing the relationship between the X variable of interest (e.g., anger, interest, inhibition/activation, etc.) and Y, a measured physiological (increased circulation, metabolism, electrical activity, etc.) or behavioral (crying, laughing, etc.) effect, as a function of controlled input (sensory/environmental or spoken/semantic) by the investigator. When these *a posteriori* cognitive responses are elicited in the absence of sensory impressions, we suspect they respond to innate or unidentified *a priori* input. So long as mathematics is a valuable language tool to represent objects/events, semantic judgments, *a priori* or not, depend on their original tangible content and not on the language tool. It should also be noticed that sensory modalities are neutral, and only the circumstantial reality of the actor can give them meaning, as registered in the output/behavior.

I had previously been warned about the technological explosion of the post-computer, late 20th-century age, and the cognitive stranglehold theoretical particle physicists had on controlling the evolution of science and natural philosophy into the 21st century. I always like to stand on solid firm grounds before my mind soars into the virtual domain of open-ended abstractions. In real life, a good car mechanic may be more important than a physics professor specializing in automotive mechanics, when it comes to fixing a damaged real car. In the study of consciousness, we have many problems to solve in the brain, even before we understand how it works. Theorizing about how the mind processes sensory input and executes an adaptive solution transcends the immediate and sets the strategy for solving ALL putative and related problems that may arise. Still, the hands-on knowledge of a mechanic/professional about the structure/function of the car/brain is required. When, upon retirement, you work alone on mind/body relationships, neither the bright logic mathematician nor the skilled neurosurgeon will be satisfactory, unless you go multidisciplinary and constantly fear spreading yourself too thin. This is better than knowing everything about the computer formulations applicable to brain dynamics by studying more and more about less and less, until asymptotically you know everything about nothing! Needing to escape my emotional pain, I took the hard multidisciplinary way. This decision required choosing the logical foundations of my "existential" approach. My conclusions would hopefully be falsifiable in the laboratory (by measurements) and/or verifiable on the metaphysical logic desk. Ideally, my judgments on self-consciousness would be of the synthetic *a posteriori* variety, leaving to mathematicians the analytic *a priori* computer processing of their symbolic/sentential logic representations, which do not require familiarity with structural/functional aspects of e.g., the amygdala, hippocampus, or cortical columns. Likewise, knowing about them but not knowing what to do with them, other than excising them or injecting some specific medication when injured, was not the solution either. We had to develop a hybrid approach, combining respective contributions into one whole unit, the epistemic-ontological unit. We needed a synthetic *a posteriori modus operandi*, based principally on empirical or contingent results of varying degrees of generality. Our species' sense-phenomenal resolution limits underdetermine sensory impressions as to their truth-value and semantic content. Consequently, the resulting judgments are based on empirical, not *a priori*, intuitions. The logical truths of analytic judgments include those possible noumenal worlds in which human experience is impossible. Their semantic content is not sensory-based, but conceptual.

It is important that we learn more about brain dynamics, about how we humans make decisions on important and relevant bio-psychosocial (BPS) issues that control the quality of our quotidian and intellectual lives, because human rationality is essentially oriented towards making continuous adjustments to optimize the outcomes of our interactivity with changing environmental influences beyond our control. Because of the self-evident biological imperative for survival of the human species, as witnessed by the spontaneous, unconscious, servo-controlled adjustments, our efforts are biased towards an anthropocentric focus, sustained primarily by meaningful and trustworthy empirical/referential data inputs. Hence, the emphasis on formulating our judgments based on synthetic *a posteriori* propositions, especially when analyzing the relevant psychosocial aspects of existence, where the results may not necessarily be applicable in all possible worlds. This is not meant to stop the search for universal synthetic *a priori* truths as a goal, when budgetary priorities are assigned. If nothing else, we unavoidably come to the conclusion that, beyond sensory phenomena, a complex structured reality "exists" that resists being reduced to logical representations. This is an entity all languages explain as being caused by an "intelligent design" without being committed to a spatiotemporal description. While natural philosophies are systematically built upon propositions whose bottom-up inputs originate from directly referential sensory attributions, perceptual data, or their conceptualized representations, our innate self-conscious faculties generate a higher-order unity that requires the consideration of an "intelligent design," as history and negentropic order testify to. Is there a non-rational or proto-rational consciousness that transcends existential reality? *Quære*!

One often wonders why anyone would insist on continuing to spend precious family time trying to explain things like life, consciousness, language acquisition and processing, brain neuronal representations of information, and their translation into inner and reportable language, etc. Is it not better to spend unpaid time during retirement in sports and entertainment or at the bar? Why this almost obsessive-compulsive search for explanations about an invisible world at both ends of a quasi-infinite spectrum? Does the mind hallucinate when burdened with an oversupply of gray matter? I also mean hallucinations on messianic ambitions or on controlling minds for universal or self-serving benefit. I never paid much attention to this slow but unrelenting drive to analyze, scrutinize, and forever find a reason or explanation for anything and everything that moves or not. This is enough to drive normal persons out of their minds, to witness on a daily basis. If not, ask my pretty wife Suzi, always solving problems in perpetual motion along the fast track of existence. All of which makes me think about what proportion of doers and thinkers society needs for survival. Can Volusia County survive without auto mechanics . . . ? No! Can it survive without experts in classical mechanics theory . . . ? Definitely yes! Should people be free to choose their hobbies after retirement? Some choose bar hopping, bed hopping, golf playing, lawn landscaping, stamp collecting, or music playing. Others choose reading, writing, cooking, or travelling. What could be wrong with marrying your computer in a joint search for invisible objects to be arbitrarily represented with letters, numbers, or words so that you can now play with them using arbitrary but convenient rules of play? Should that be considered a hobby or psychopathological behavior? Should we be saved from psychic self-destruction . . . ?

Finally, we anticipate that future conceptual developments will consider abandoning the frustrating efforts of reconciliation/harmonization between the physical brain and metaphysical mind domains, and declare them instead ". . . independent, non-interacting worlds, and just consider how cooperatively we can synchronize their independent 'activities' so that, epistemologically, by becoming 'entangled' we can formulate an algorithm explaining how we transform the non-linear physical world into the linear sequence of events that our senses functionally experience as reality. Enter a conceptual 'time,' this time as an 'emergent' phenomenon. We do this by manipulating tensor space mathematics to cancel the effects of the temporal asymmetry nature tries to impose on us. We leave out the mathematical elaboration of the possible formulations for future discussions."

12 Quo Vadis Evolution? The Immanent Invariant and the Transcendental Transforming Horizons

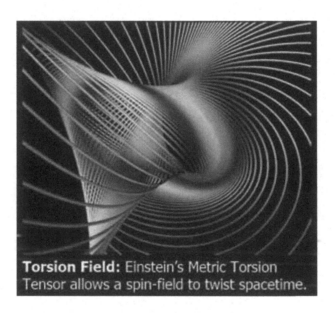

Torsion Field: Einstein's Metric Torsion Tensor allows a spin-field to twist spacetime.

INTRODUCTION

At some point in our lives we all have experienced and enjoyed the immense pleasure of an introspective, self conscious trip into ourselves, a kind of self-induced solitary confinement from the surrounding crowds, trying to ponder on the physically invariant aspects of our individualized existential reality, the **what** of 'I' vis a vis 'the other', i.e., trying to explain to yourself why some things do change while others apparently remain the same, wondering **how** you got where you are and **where** will you go, if anywhere, **when** you . . . . and everyone else die, quo vadis? More often than not you feel overwhelmed by the super complexity of the physical sensory phenomena reaching consciousness, not to mention the equally experienced qualia originating from the extrasensory/metaphysical object or event invisible to our direct sensory detection or measurement. Then, in frustration, you conclude that 'the more things change, the more they remain the same', "vivir es ver volver" (life is to see same things past come back)? But, if you are afflicted by the 'sane psychosis' of curiosity, then you make it a hobby to meditate deep about the **why,** using whatever information resources, whatever science, technology and metaphysical logic has been placed within your reach. But the conclusions are disappointing when we find out that other subhuman species enjoy lower thresholds to the same sensory information and we discover that our human brain natural combinatorial capacity without the aid of instruments is dismally low.

Yet, we all witness the self-evident truths about the Newtonian apple falling to the ground, rain water streaming down hill, the loss of structure and/or function of complex objects falling from high buildings or contrariwise, the required supply of externally applied energy or effort to make same object move or spontaneously restructure itself when returning to its original locus in the tall building. A closer look will immediately evidence that complexly structured objects or events exhibit either a bilateral or rotational symmetry, the kind of ordered complexity that was never the result of natural spontaneous processes. On the other hand, the loss of order and complexity, as when a tall building naturally collapses, brings all systems to a minimum of free energy and a corresponding increase in entropy. Then we observe, with Pierre Curie, that the symmetry elements of the causes must be found in their effects while the converse is not true, i.e., the effects can be more symmetric than the causes. Is evolution fueled by asymmetry, induced by external forces or spontaneous?

Then we wonder like Leibniz did in his 'Principle of Sufficient Reason' (PSR): Why so? Then we also naturally posit the intervention of an efficient causal agency as the driving force behind this transformational change in the direction of a lesser entropy content (negentropy) and increased organizational complexity. If there is no **sufficient reason** for one thing to happen instead of another, the Leibniz principle says that nothing will happen and the initial situation will not change. What then is the efficient causal agency in defiance of natural laws and why? Where in infinity or transfinity is this agency located? Maybe inside our own human brains? If the latter, since it cannot spontaneously come into being, where—if anywhere—is the external source of inspirational righteousness originating the information being transferred to our decisional human brain lobe?

The simplest way to start digging into this analysis is to postpone the identification of the source and start with the relatively easier chore of characterizing the kind of information being transferred . . . . or settle for the complex structural/functional evolutionary changes resulting therefrom? To differentiate the constituent elements of complexity we notice, prima facie, order in structure and function of either single sensory objects or in situations where interacting sensory objects describe a measurable event. This is the proper domain of the 4-d ontological aspect of the scientific methodology. But much beyond the reaches of this Minkowsky spatio—temporal domain we find the equally relevant epistemological n-1 d metaphysical logic to assist in the explanation of that experienced force which cannot be described experimentally as a physical object or observable event. To follow is a brief exposition of the need for a hybrid epistemontological approach when analyzing existential reality where symmetry considerations play a decisive role in the human brain when processing the information input when ordering the complexities of physical and metaphysical reality.

ARGUMENTATION

We notice that most sensory objects have in common a given symmetry, either a bilateral symmetry (e.g., two arms of a human body statue in anatomical position) or a rotational symmetry (e.g., spherical objects) where there is complete equivalence between the existing alternatives (the left hand with respect to the right hand or a full 360 degree axial rotation of a human statue/spherical object, respectively). As in nature, we also notice that, in the absence of an asymmetric transforming cause (externally applied or self-induced force?), the initial invariant state symmetry is preserved, i.e., a breaking of the original symmetry—whether human-induced or in its highest natural entropy state—cannot happen without a reason because *an asymmetry cannot originate spontaneously*. How then was microscopic and cosmological order 'created'? A tall order for the scientific community to handle with its methodology, imagine now the level of complexity faced when you consider the invariance under a specified group of transformations and the symmetry concept is now applied not only to ontological spatial statues or spherical objects but also to relevant epistemologically abstract virtual 'objects' such as found in metaphysical logic math expressions, e.g., dynamical equations of state.

But the curious mind has to start from the sense-phenomenal physically obvious to the statistically probable, metaphysically inferred and then the theosophically possible explanations model when the effort has exceeded the human brain capacities to epistemontologically hybridize and harmonize all the different elements in the first two as a coherent unit or unitary whole. An extraordinary task when you have to consider the constitutive elements in a single human being made up of trillions of microscopic living cells, the majority of which of different species and each, not only following their individualized trajectories through the Many World universes according to the idiosyncrasies of their many molecules, atoms, subatomic particles, etc., but also tracking the evolutionary path of the unit human life to its ultimate destination. Yet you are able to maintain through life the 'singularity' of your unit body and mind as it invariantly persist while changing. In other words, you are simultaneously a statistically invariant, physico-chemical **you** and a constantly transforming **many**, while you traverse a world line in one or many universes . . . . going somewhere.

So, historically we start by a classification of sensory reality according to their varied symmetry, structural macro properties as manifested in harmony, beauty, and unity followed by their inferred micro structural properties after their epistemological translation into irreducible representations of their fundamental physical symmetry groups, e.g., a group-theoretical account of objects or their canonical Hamiltonian representation as dynamic entities. The next step was to harmonize the invariant geometrical abstractions with the dynamic Hamiltonian equations of motion. The complex evolving dynamic theories of nature were made easier to comprehend by Jacobi with the strategy of applying transformations of the dynamic variables that leave the Hamiltonian equations invariant. This way the original formulation became thereby transformed into a new one that is simpler but perfectly equivalent albeit somewhat removed from the existential reality it purports to substitute for. May this be carrying symmetry principles too far, the reason why general relativity and quantum physics cannot be integrated into a unit theory and allow both to reconcile. We briefly analyzed this constrain in a previous chapter.

From both an *ontological* and epistemological perspective, symmetries in theories represent properties existing in nature that characterize the structure and function of the physical world as illustrated by their methodological success in predicting the existence of new particles in physics, e.g., the prediction of the W and Z particles in the unification of the weak and electromagnetic interactions. Of course some symmetries are observed while others are only inferred and thus validated by their predictive value. It would seem as if symmetries represent natural, minimum free energy states in equilibrium. As such they serve the purpose of being used as constraints on the evolution of new physical theories, a valuable normative role assuring the compatibility of quantities, dimensions and form in their constitutive equations. This is especially important now while we struggle to find a unified description of all the fundamental forces of nature (gravitational, weak, electromagnetic and strong) in terms of underlying local symmetry groups. Hopefully the unification is just as credible at the explicit, measurable, ontological level as it may be at the implicit representational/epistemological levels, i.e., observably invariant global space time symmetry and the inferred locally varying continuous symmetry. In our opinion all symmetry principles are operational transcendental strategies aimed at making our understanding of the world more intelligible with no guarantee of reaching reality 'in se'. But, there is indeed a natural connection between the invariables and structural realism just like between symmetry and *objectivity,* the validity of which is predicated on being the same for all observers and do not depend on any particular perspective under which is being considered. Objective realism is that which remains invariant no matter how many transformations it suffered when forced into a convenient reference frame. Can we make the same claim for what seems the human-contrived epistemological explanations of transfinite dynamic invisibilities 'existing' beyond the human 4-d spatiotemporal Minkowsky cage?

Why did the human species historically and conveniently choose the invariant features of symmetry to explain his dynamic evolution through space time? Was it unconsciously genetically/biologically determined, subconsciously mimetically/psychosocially imposed by circumstantial/environmental constraints or is it the inevitable consequence of the freely willed, self conscious effort of a few historical prophets inspired by transfinite 'revelations' guiding their efforts through the pathways of righteousness to preserve life, psychic comfort and social conviviality, i.e., create and sustain a biopsychosocial (BPS) equilibrium through life? The common denominator found in a BPS equilibrium is 'symmetry', whether discovered or invented in the mathematical proportions and harmonies they contain, or the related properties and beauty of their form. A combination of an essential biological, life preserving effort and the convenience of a happy psychosocial environment in guarantee of the survival of human life and self consciousness. The symmetric proportions of material objects not only have an esthetic appeal (beauty, regularity and unity) but, when deliberately designed by the architect or engineer as e.g., the regular polygons, polyhedrals, etc. as the structural foundations of buildings, factories, etc., the geometry is defined in terms of their invariance under specified groups of rotations and reflections, not necessarily esthetic criteria. No wonder the current appeal of differential geometry and topology to theoretical physicists when explaining the invisible domain of relevant sub atomic and cosmological reality. This time symmetry considerations propitiated the development of group-theoretic representations that have been so useful in modern physics to create 'equivalent groups' by symmetry transformations easier to exchange with one another without allegedly substantially changing the unit wholeness being considered. In our opinion, this may introduce non-compatible elements into general formulations affecting their claimed invariance under the transformation when equivalent elements are exchanged according to one of the specified mathematical operations, as the case may be. Having perhaps reached the limits of human instrumental resolution in the description of objects or phenomena, we have now emphasized more the application of *symmetry principles* to natural laws in our attempt to achieve a *unity of different and equal elements* in our explanations/conceptualizations of reality which has become central to modern physics. There are always serious problems when you hybridize invariant symmetry principles with transforming symmetry arguments into a unit whole theory.

SUMMARY AND CONCLUSIONS

Needless to say, the professions of medicine, law and engineering practitioners have been more efficient in doing their 'thing' than their academic philosophy equivalents in the same areas because the former are mostly dealing with the ontologically and statistically invariant macro aspects of 4-d space time reality while the latter must conceptually keep simultaneous control of both invariant and transforming aspects of real time existential and virtual universal models of the same reality. The application of symmetry principles has provided ontology and epistemology useful tools to discover the structure and function of absolute reality, all within the known perceptual and conceptual limitations of the human observer to find/identify noumenal reality.

The most successful efforts in that direction have been to control the dynamic Hamiltonian formulations of measurable phenomena by conveniently holding them as invariant by the use of transforming operations of the relevant variables in the dynamic equations (Jacobian transforms). This way the intractable dynamics are transformed into simpler but perfectly equivalent now amenable to to combine, permute, exchange with equivalent representations, etc. Whether this simplification correspond to reality, quare!

We have dramatize the complexity of reality by reminding the reader that the historical, lifetime chronology of a single living human being is a macro statistical description conveniently ignoring the concomitant evolutionary path of trillions of microscopic living entities, mostly of different subhuman species, e.g., bacteria, molds, etc., each cell, molecule, atom, subatomic particle, etc following independent trajectories through the various Multiverse options. Yet the unitary integrity of your physical body and mental idiosyncrasies remain distinguishable whether you traverse a world line in one universe, or many.

Because of the successful influence of symmetry principles in scientific methodology pursuits, as outlined above, we do not appreciate as much its impact on the metaphysical logic of our explanatory models of existential and abstract/virtual reality equivalents. We briefly discussed two outstanding influences, the Leibnizean Principle of Sufficient Reason (PSR) and Pierre Curie's theory of causality. PSR stresses the correlation between symmetry (bilateral or rotational) and natural stability implied in the complete equivalence between the existing alternatives, as discussed above, e.g., if the alternative positions are equivalent why choose among them (invariance). This means that in the absence of an asymmetric efficient cause there is no reason to change, i.e., a breaking of the initial symmetry cannot happen without a reason, or *an asymmetry cannot originate spontaneously* without defying laws of nature, yet it happens, as argued.

In a related argument, Pierre Curie, argues that the symmetry elements of the causes must be found in their effects while the converse is not true, i.e., the effects can be more symmetric than the causes. And we ask: is evolution fueled by asymmetry, induced by external forces or spontaneous?

As a parting 'lei motif' coda allow me to philosophize a little on what I have tried to market in the previous chapters of these volumes: "The Hypothetical 'How' Integrating the What, Where, When, Who and Why of the Constitutive Elements of 4-d Human Existential Reality."

This brief exposition could have been entitled "Reciprocal Information transfer between human species and n-dimensional space.", or "From here to eternity and back." for that matter. It naturally follows from my two previous chapters on 'intraspecies' and 'interspecies' information transfer respectively. Within the contextual guidelines of the 'epistemontological hybrid, biopsychosocial (BPS) model, the 'what' refers to the information content (matter, energy) whether ontologically *described* in its intraspecies transition from sensory receptors to consciousness or epistemologically *explained* as it reciprocally travels to and fro man and n-dimensional space. The rest is my sheer wishful thinking poetry. The expressions are ontologically rooted on *observables* from the scientific methodology arsenal and on epistemological inferences from metaphysical logic axioms/tautologies where reduction to symbolic or sentential logic representations has been deliberately reduced here to a minimum to reach all informed audiences. The 'epistemontological' hybrid approach will become obvious if we can imagine the linear temporal transition of either a visible sphere or a line in our real-time Minkosky 4-d macro space as these structures sequentially halve their dimension until they escape unaided sensory or instrumental detection (from magnifying glass to electron microscopy). As the *described* features of 'what' enter an invisible extrasensory domain we have no reason to believe it has existentially disappeared (as long as we 'sense' its relevant effects) simply because we may have to resort now to *explanations* as to its probable presence somewhere in space. While it may originally sound counterintuitive, it is not difficult to imagine, e.g., the basketball size becoming a softball size, a tennis ball, a ping-pong ball, a marble size, etc. until it eventually becomes a zero dimensional point singularity, invisible to us because it has transcended/escaped our sense detection inside our 4-d sense-phenomenal state. Same argument applies to the visible line—or any other geometry imaginable—transition towards a spherical point singularity. Likewise we can imagine a not so linear, stepwise and reversible sequential flow of information projecting from different geometries inside or outside our sensory sphere of detection (which we conveniently may represent as 3 dimensions of space xyz and one of time) to form our 4-d Minkowsky sensory world. We can either choose 3 lines diverging from same origin 'o' at right angles to each other or use spherical coordinates inside a geodesic. This reverse flow of information arriving eventually to a particular receptor as a zero-dimensional quantum energy unit sphere (wave) to and fro all of space or hyperspace, whether relevant or not to the human species quotidian experience carries important information to our environment. Upon arrival it will release its energy content on any particle, atom, molecular, cellular, tissue, organ or macrostructure containing/vibrating at the appropriate phase and resonant frequency energy that makes coupling/entanglement and transmission of information possible, e.g., an incomplete electron orbit in a vibrating atom/molecule inside a DNA spiral, photosynthetic chromophores or wiggling protein string receptors. At the brain level this entanglement or collapse of the wave function with all appropriate receptor configurations provides the background noise waves we described earlier in the EEG responsible for amplification of subthreshold energy transfer (intra and interspecies) from the internal/external environment.

There are many—obvious and not so obvious—geometrical reasons why information (matter/energy, particle/wave) should travel optimally as spherical quanta but we find it mathematically convenient to represent their transient location using spherical coordinates or inside a 3-d (xyz) cubical space to be able to answer the 'where' question about the spatio-temporal position of the 'what' wave/particle (wavicle) in a given moment in time either inside or outside our sensory/visible or extrasensory/invisible domain or manifold. Notice that any geometry, e.g., polygon, is a sphere in potency as it sequentially diminishes its size, as discussed.

If we stretch our imagination it should not be difficult to visualize that, as the pure energy content E diminishes in the smallest spherical massless quantum, a particle M will be created from the condensate according to the correlation between mass and energy given by E= MC2. A dimensionless sphere singularity 'a' has unit 'matter'/information moving to and fro across space and hyperspace until detected or otherwise captured by an appropriate resonant receptor, visual, olfactory, audible or otherwise.

Consider now how, in locating 'a''s matter/energy ('what') photon singularity's position in space, we can also increase its information content and, from an assumed linear trajectory, identify a second point 'b' along its path at variable distances from its origin 'o'. The resulting *line* can now provide information about positions (its own/another object) along such 'ab' line as it extends into or returns from n-d space by developing a uni-dimensional linear algebra. By adding a third point 'c' outside line ab we create a 2-d plane and, by measuring the angle sustained as the line rotates from the origin 'o' (e.g., at 'a' or 'b') to reach the third point 'c'. Now we are creating a vector calculus to explain the position of a wavicle in both the previous 2-d plane or the new 3-d world scenario more consistent with our sense-phenomenal reality experience. Now we continue to add information on 'where' by indicating how far and in what direction either point 'c' or any other object along the line crossing line 'oc' as it extends into or returns from n-d space—whether inside the 3-d sensory box/geodesic or beyond.

Notice also that this way, yet another visible or invisible point/object 'd' need not be either on the 2-d xy plane created (embedded above or below it) or along the oà'c' line to be identified. If so, by extending a line from 'o' to 'c' we have created a third dimension z, improving on our ability to describe any point/object 'd' location *anywhere* inside new 3-d space created or in hyperspace (as long as being possibly detected along line 'od', unless another 3-d/geodesic is subsequently created with point 'd' as the new origin), i.e., this way we can create additional location units in space and hyperspace as long as the complexity of the required analytical algebras and computing resources do not get unwieldy, e.g., by extending a line from 'c' → 'd', 'd' → 'e', etc.

Depending on the object/point distance from the original reference point 'o' we can develop the algebras describing the time unit increments to get from point to point or line to line, sphere to sphere, etc. and, by describing how fast ('t') an object covers that distance D, we invent the concepts of Velocity = dD/t and acceleration = dV/dt and thereby increase the information content on the 'where' is the matter/energy 'what' is coming from or going to and incorporating it in our concept of a 4-d spatiotemporal unit sphere a la Minkowsky. Having accepted the convenience of this unit of localization 'where' we are also describing the 'when' as the time element gets incorporated into the 3-d space dimension. Of course the 'what' need not be sitting static waiting to be identified, it can be dynamically spinning on an axis, rotating with precessional movements, revolving, etc. where each change in the position of a given point requires the appropriate analytical construction of the suggested 4-d or geodesic unit. To illustrate, in a 4-d space, a vector displays a particular behavior when acted upon by a rotation or when reflected in a plane surface. Such spatial rotations and reflections provide additional information about the causal dynamics and are best expressed in differential geometry representations using Lie or Clifford algebras to describe the complex geometry in terms of spinors (Seeorientationentanglement at http://en.wikipedia.org/wiki/Orientation_entanglement).

It should be noticed that the implication of a trajectory of unit matter/energy is linear along the straight lines joining 2 points or restricted to lines lying on the 2 surfaces of planes formed by joining 3 points or the interior/exterior surfaces or inside the interior volumes of the 3d structures formed when leaving the 2-d plane surface. We know that measured experimental trajectories, e.g., along the surface area of a 2-d plane, may show maxima/minima variations along a 1-d line (on the plane) before reaching its destination, e.g., recursive cycles that when moving along a straight line appear as sine waves in a Fourier analysis, etc., and that these trajectories vary according to the influence of other *adjacent* locations along its path.

Yet, it should not be difficult to see the convenience of representing any point/object location *anywhere* in n-d space as a localized 4-d Minkowsky space using spherical coordinates for analytical purposes. The task is being able to trace the path of its origin and/or destiny After all a spherical adimensional point singularity represents the hypothetical origin/end of a reversible transmission of matter/energy wavicles between 2 locations anywhere in n-d space which can evolve from a massless energy source into an integrated traveling, invisible wavicle in hyperspace or the visible object inside our sensory 4-d space by the accretion of coincident points entangling by resonant phase coupling or otherwise, i.e., any multidimensional object or adimensional singularity can transmit its constitutive information (mass/energy content) by differentiation/integration into simpler/complex units of transfer approaching as a limit the unit spherical quantum configuration or the observable object as the case may be. This way, the visible transmitter differentiates into quantum spherical units for projections traveling at speeds exceeding the speed of light into new locations inside sensory 4-d space and beyond while the receiver receptor(s) integrate(s) the information units into new visible objects in space or hyperspace by resonant phase coupling entanglement.

The most fascinating result of this model of matter/energy information transfer is that it allows for an analysis/understanding of a few other counterintuitive albeit self-evident observable facts in apparent violation of natural laws as will briefly be expanded below, e.g., negentropy as seen in the synthesis of order out of disorder when making conscious free will decisions. The reversible energy/mass information transfer to and fro between a source and its receptor destination seems to be characterized as being a quantum/discontinued, non-linear, non local, asymmetric but **not necessarily** an energy dissipating entropic event as witnessed by self-evident sense-phenomenal and historical manifestations, e.g., spontaneous and self-sustained cosmic/institutional order and life generation. Hence the paradox of two co-existing systems, a visible deterministic *described* by the scientific methodology and an invisible indeterministic *explained* by metaphysic logic; a probable world, held indelibly together by the probabilities of quantum theory provisions—in a hybrid indelible epistemontological unit. This cognitive approach makes possible a different view of existential reality as an equilibrium between the biological, psychic and social survival imperatives tailored to individualized complex circumstantial factors in the biosphere niche. In the process it opens the doors ajar for further explorations on the possibility of modeling a new physics to explain the mesoscopic quantum world by integrating the input contributions originating from many vital body sources (neuro-endocrine, immune, genetic, etc.) and/or n-d space. This would be the result of viewing the reversible transition between the micro subplanckian level and the macro cosmological n-d level via the visible 4-d mesoscopic level as resulting from the integration of invisible Planck constant quantum units of matter/energy and/or volumes as they reach or leave macro quantum phases to reach visible levels of identification using same mathematical transfer strategies as discussed. This possibility comes as the result of analyzing the information/energy transfer across domains/manifolds as discussed under quantum transfer of Planck units (constants) and now viewed as the possibility of dealing in addition with massive but invisible dark matter in our midst. This view is made possible when we briefly examine further what was explained above about the new manifolds appearing as we transcend (symmetry breaking) the 4-d space constraints into micro or macro hyperspace. Some have characterized these adjacent levels as onion peels, layered sheaths, Bohr orbitals, etc. of space-time units. Could the convergence of these many massless unit singularities (or biophoton aggregates thereof) on brain matter constitute the invisible supercomplex mind state? Quare.

Our quotidian existential reality, as experienced in the ecosystem niche of our biosphere, gets individually configured inside an ordinary 4-d space-time sensory reality and the attending biopsychosocial circumstances as described mostly by the natural sciences. Yet we know there is more to it than meets the eye that influences our decision-making process, especially our psychic and social behavior details . . . things that defy rationality and common sense at times. Well, it so happens that we find similar conclusions stemming from the results we see when playing around with mathematical logic, things like imaginary lines going back to infinity, non locality, a particle being in 2 different locations simultaneously, etc. What we must remember is that our human species has limited capacity for the sensory resolution of 'real' objects/events even inside our ordinary 4-d space, not to mention the limitations in brain combinatorial capacity to analyze variables exceeding a limited number of objects or events even though their shape/form or location are invisible they somehow may substantially influence our daily lives. Enter metaphysics to complete the reality picture. The strictly human features allowing these cognitive incursions into the invisible domains are our ability for introspective search for self and our language ability to describe how we differ from others as expressed/represented in logic symbols or sentences. Man is back at the center of the universe, a neo-Copernican revolution?

First we observe that an infinite regression in size of any geometrical 3-d structure comes to a spherical point, visible in our unaided 4-d reality or not. Then we realize that in the reverse sequence material geometries probably started with a point also, visible or not! We have tentatively 'discovered' 'how' the essence of the 'what' has ontological descriptions and epistemological explanatory inferences about their presence, especially when outside the sensory 4-d reality. Then we form a line by joining 2 points and we discover 'how' we can represent the probable location ('where') of that invisible point if located along the 1-d extension of the line 'from here to eternity'. If outside that line, I form another line by joining 3 points to form a 2-d plane surface where it may be located along any line contained inside (above or below) the 2 surfaces formed. As mentioned above, we can develop a vector calculus to locate any point on the plane by, e.g., measuring the angular displacement of 2 intersecting lines with a common origin. We can develop a plane geometry to improve on the localization ('where') of any point ('what') in that surface, e.g., Euclidean geometry, Pythagoras theorem, etc. We have improved our localization of matter/energy from a line 'scalar' to a "vector" field. Now an unexpected result surfaces as we discover that, from the innocent x2+y2=c2 relationship between the triangular intersecting lines at right angle formed by the 3 points, we discover not only the geometric functions (sine, cosine, etc.) when the plane is a circle but the counterintuitive notions of infinity, recursive cycles, negative numbers, imaginary and complex numbers, etc., all by manipulating the symbolic representations! However, an object in a vector field can change strength and direction when acting as a source or can experience them as a destination, e.g., a migratory bird in flight under the effects of earth's gravitational field when the strength and distance of the field varies as a function of time.

If we now want to locate a point 'z' located **outside** the plane (above or below) we extend a line from a point origin on the xy plane to z creating in the process a 3-d cubical unit space or unit sphere (geodesical) as explained in solid and space geometries thus creating our unit 4-d space that enables us to trace and thus *explain* the probable origin/destination or location of matter/energy sources or destinations of at least unit spherical singularities which can be further geometrically embellished to accommodate other degrees of freedom emerging in their trajectory and resulting from internal/external influences, e.g., tensor and spinor fields that better explains the dynamics of forces acting at a distance and hoping to better explain the phenomenon of cosmological 'non-locality' of the Einstenian 'spooky actions at a distance'. When the bird flies in a straight line scalar the vector becomes a 0-order tensor but when other influences (describable also as vectors) come into play, the order of the tensor increases depending on the number of participating vectors in a given space-time location. Any number of the 5 known forces in nature (gravity, electricity, magnetism, etc.) and their strength at a given point in space-time (when explained as vectors) are then represented as the elements of a particular matrix for analytical and evaluation purposes without defining the type/nature of influence being considered, gravitational or otherwise. It is important to realize that each participating force creates its own time-line that can either coincide or intersect others and thus creating thereby 3 additional dimensions of time for a 6-d hyperspace, without including other time-lines generated by other rotational forces present (spin, precession, wobbling, etc.) all possibly being integrated in our BPS model into a resultant 'existential' location inside an expanded, real-time unit 4-d space.

So much for this brief orientation on the probable location ('where') of the matter/energy ('what') participating in the dynamic synthesis/degradation at a given moment in time ('when') of that 4-d sense-phenomenal view we refer to as our human existential reality. But the unit 4-d sphere concatenation of n-d locations model cannot now, if ever, explain/identify the force behind the reversible flow of energy/matter between us and others across n-d space, the 'who' and 'why' of existential reality. These answers we leave to poets and theologians who provide evolving transitory palliatives to substitute for the unreachable and invisible Omega point(s) at either infinite 'end' of the reversible flow along the dis-continuum path. The easy answer is to dismiss it as, "it's all in your head". No brain, no reality, no consciousness. Maybe for us pitiful humans, life is not about having arrived but about getting there as we travel along an asymptotic path . . .

A long time ago I was impressed when I observed in my biophysics lab at Sloan Kettering Institute in New York the sequential transformation of elongated chick embryo fibroblasts grown in cultures to spherical invasive cancer cells by just adding a white powder (Rous Sarcoma virus) from a test tube to the Petri Dish! I was determined to explain how an inanimate ribonucleotide molecule can be animated to invade and infect and transform other normal cells as observed with the electron microscope. Rubin and Temin modeled what I couldn't see and won them a Nobel prize, the ribonucleotide virus had become associated with the host's DNA! Later on I was again perplexed to record brain activity from implanted electrodes in a hungry cat's reticular mesencephalic area isolated from any possibility of sensory input (blinded, in a positive pressure cage in a closed room). This happened when either food or another cat from the opposite sex approached from afar! In another setting, I was able to call the attention of a lady sitting in front of me during a conference, almost at will. I couldn't wait to retire and work on these spooky experiences. Years of study and three volumes on "Neurophilosophy of Consciousness" published later I still have not been able to explain, let alone describe, the identity of the 'who' if any or the mysterious 'why'. One often wonders what would be the result of an experimental paradigm shift emphasizing on man as the center and reason for all things existing, in the visible sense-phenomenal 4-d and the invisible, extrasensory n-d domains. Perhaps if we become committed to spend (or waste) time studying/exploring those intangible imaginary numbers, non-local actions at a distance, negative time, simultaneous presence of one particle in two locations, information transfer at the speed of light, dark matter and other invisibilities we will move closer to Omega along the asymptotic line . . . For starters, concentrate on the mesoscopic level and trace the conceptual path of an invisible Planck's energy quantum singularity as it builds up by accretion into the sense reality of the mesoscopic level where dark matter considerations will probably show its need of inclusion. It may not be far-fetched that the probable explanation of the unit 4-d existential reality will be formulated in terms of scaled-up/scaled-down subsets of unit mass/ energy quantum content reversibly traveling to and fro the extreme ends of micro and cosmic reality as the dark/fractal hierarchies become distinguishable/detected inside our existential, sense-phenomenal 4-d mesoscopic reality.

End of Book.